The Industrial Heritage of
HAMPSHIRE
and the
ISLE OF WIGHT

Dovecote at Lainston House near Winchester.

The Industrial Heritage of
HAMPSHIRE
and the
ISLE OF WIGHT

Pam Moore

Phillimore

1988

Published by
PHILLIMORE & CO. LTD.
Shopwyke Hall, Chichester, Sussex

ISBN 085033 665 1

Printed in Great Britain by
by Richard Clay Ltd.,
Bungay, Suffolk

For my parents, Bob and Phyllis Spencer,
with love and gratitude

Contents

List of Maps

List of Illustrations

Illustration Acknowledgements

The author is grateful to the following for permission to reproduce the illustrations: Frith postcards, 3; E. Course, 2, 8, 10, 17, 20, 21, 30, 37, 42, 49, 53, 67, 70, 75, 81, 82, 86, 89, 92, 98; R. Mapp, 59; D. Plunkett, 5; S. Shrimpton, University of Southampton, 26; B. Sprunt, 44, 45, 46, 47; F. G. O. Stuart, 1. All the remaining photographs were taken by the author.

Acknowledgements

I became interested in history as a teenager, thanks mainly to an excellent teacher, Miss Muriel Chapman; I shall be forever in her debt. My study became more specialised during my period of employment in Portsmouth Dockyard, when I was fascinated by the remarkable industrial buildings all around me. Whilst attending Fareham Technical College I met Peter Singer who introduced me to industrial archaeology as a discipline, and subsequent courses under the direction of Ray Riley and Edwin Course led me to devote more time to the study of industrial heritage. I am grateful to them all.

Many people have contributed to this book in some way. Those who have kindly allowed me to use their photographs are acknowledged separately; Rosemary Shearer drew the maps, and I am grateful to Ray Riley, both for general advice and encouragement, and for assistance with the planning of the cartography for this book.

I am indebted to Edwin Course, and to many members of the Southampton University Industrial Archaeology Group, for information used in the text, and for assistance with fieldwork. Special thanks are due to David Alderton and to my father, both of whom read my manuscript and offered constructive criticism and advice. Many friends have encouraged me in this project, including Kerry Edwards, Rodney Hall, Ingela Liwang, Kath and Ron Mapp, Marilyn Palmer and Phil Turner; also a number of colleagues in industrial archaeological circles. My parents have been most supportive throughout.

My text should present an accurate picture as at March 1988; for any errors or omissions, I alone am responsible.

Chapter One

Introduction

Dr. Angus Buchanan wrote more than a decade and a half ago that 'Industrial Archaeology has become a popular subject . . . because it offers something for everybody. It is concerned with that common heritage of the people of Britain, their shared past, and in particular with the outstanding national achievement of the last two centuries'.[1] Until about thirty years ago, there was only very limited interest in our industrial past and the study of its remains; today the subject is explored on television and in books; in evening classes and through industrial archaeology societies all over the country. Despite the reservations of some practitioners of the subject about the use of the term 'industrial archaeology', an increasing number of people are becoming aware of what it stands for, and are showing an interest in learning about it. As Dr. Neil Cossons points out, 'The Industrial Revolution in Britain which gained momentum during the middle years of the eighteenth century and dominated the nineteenth, was a unique phenomenon in the history of mankind, the repercussions of which have spread throughout the world'.[2] We have every reason to be proud of this part of our history, and the study of our industrial heritage is indeed a worthy pursuit. This can be confined to superficial study, resulting in an increasing awareness of our surroundings, or can be pursued in depth - say of a particular facet of the subject, such as watermills or canals.

This book is intended to introduce the reader to the nature and scope of the industrial heritage of Hampshire and the Isle of Wight, and, it is hoped, to encourage further study. The area has frequently been regarded by industrial archaeologists and historians as a rural backwater, insignificant in the study of Britain's economic development. In the 18th century, Daniel Defoe dismissed Hampshire industry, saying that there was not 'any considerable manufacture in all this part of England'.[3] Most economic history textbooks concentrate on the 'industrial north', implying that southern England was almost entirely rural, contributing little to the industrial revolution. Whilst it would not be reasonable to suggest that Hampshire and the Isle of Wight contained heavily industrialised areas similar to, say, the Black Country, or the textile manufacturing centres in Lancashire and Yorkshire, they do have a distinctive economic history, and many relics of this have survived, thus giving the area a fascinating industrial heritage.

The physical character of both Hampshire and the Isle of Wight has had a marked influence on their economic development. The Isle of Wight's history has been governed to a large degree by its island status, resulting in the development of a number of industries on a small scale. Until recent times, with improvements in transport, it achieved a high measure of self-sufficiency, and this is evident in the remains of industry which have survived.

Hampshire benefited from having a long stretch of coastline, punctuated by harbours, which, in the age before rail transport and serviceable roads, resulted in much of the county's economic activity being linked to maritime pursuits. Shipbuilding has always been of importance, and one of Hampshire's special industries, that of defence supply, developed mainly because of the nature of Portsmouth Harbour. Southampton's natural qualities as a port, recognised for centuries, have also been important, and it is not surprising that a major dock complex dealing with both passengers and cargo grew up there.

The geographical position of both Hampshire and the Isle of Wight, with long stretches of coast, meant that inland waterways were never of great significance, as they were in

1

landlocked counties. The Isle of Wight had no canals, and those on mainland Hampshire were not very successful and were fairly short-lived.

Without doubt, the most important 'industry' in the area was agriculture, but as will be described in more detail in Chapter Two, even the type of farming practised varied in different parts of the county. In the north the downs provided an ideal location for large farms, used mainly as pasture for sheep, whilst the smaller farms of south Hampshire concentrated on a mixture of arable cultivation and market gardening. Both types of farms were to be found on the Isle of Wight.

1.   Woodmill, Southampton.

Not surprisingly, both Hampshire and the Isle of Wight supported the usual industries needed for the local population, such as brewing and corn milling. There are, however, some surprising remains of the area's industrial past - one would not, for example, expect to find a former lace factory in the centre of Newport, Isle of Wight, nor a still flourishing silk mill at Whitchurch in the north of Hampshire. The area is not noted for textile production, and to some extent it is a mystery why a few silk manufacturers settled in Hampshire; not just at Whitchurch, but in other towns such as Winchester. A possible answer lies in a factor also responsible for the growth of another Hampshire industry - paper-making. The county became a refuge for a number of Huguenots and other Protestants fleeing from persecution in Europe in the late 17th century, and this influx had an impact on its economic development.

The transport heritage of an area should not be ignored by industrial archaeologists, and in this respect Hampshire and the Isle of Wight differ somewhat. The island has always relied on sea, and occasionally air, transport to link it to the rest of Great Britain. Its internal transport network does, however, have an interesting history. The narrow roads

2. Smithy, Hook village, 1908.

3. Ventnor, Isle of Wight.

Ventnor, Isle of Wight.

with their steep gradients ensured a place of importance in the past for the railways, and it is noteworthy that the island had, at one time, three railway companies operating services.

Hampshire's transport history is very complex since, in addition to the provision of links between various centres in the county, it has always, in different ways, handled through traffic. The port of Southampton is, of course, an obvious example of this, but it is significant that the first turnpike opened in the county in 1710 linked Portsmouth, with its naval and military connections, with London.

In general, Hampshire and the Isle of Wight have never been centres for heavy industry, although there have been some exceptions. For example, Eastleigh developed around the railway workshops, with most of its settlement dating from the late 19th and early 20th centuries, when the London and South Western Railway's Carriage and Wagon Works, and Locomotive Works moved from London. Similarly, Taskers of Andover manufactured agricultural equipment, and Armfields of Ringwood had a national reputation as mill-wrights.

Such industries as coal mining, or the extraction of metalliferous ores do not figure in the area's industrial history, although some iron ore was to be found in the extreme south west of Hampshire. Iron processing, another activity rarely linked to the rural south, occurred, mainly on a small scale. As a consequence of certain inventions taking place locally, however, it has found a place in Hampshire's, and indeed the nation's, history.

Salt manufacture by evaporation was important at one time both on the Isle of Wight and in Hampshire, although today the relics of this once important industry are scanty.

As in most areas, remains of the traditional entertainment industry - the theatre and the cinema - survive. Perhaps more unusual are survivals of another aspect: the Victorian Seaside resort. Southsea, in Hampshire, still has some traditional features, but it is the Isle of Wight which has much more to offer, with towns like Ventnor retaining much of their character and charm.

Hampshire and the Isle of Wight have a very distinctive and fascinating industrial heritage, and it is hoped that, in the chapters which follow, it will be possible, as it is explored in greater depth, to indicate its infinite variety. The bibliography (Appendix 1) should enable the further study of particular facets; Appendix 2 is a list of local museums with items of special interest, and of industrial archaeological sites open to the public. One point which should be emphasised is that, if a site is on private property, the owner should be approached in advance for permission to view.

Those who may be encouraged by this book to engage in more active participation in industrial archaeology are referred to the address list in Appendix 3 which will assist them in obtaining details of national and local organisations.

Chapter Two
Agriculture and Fishing

Although frequently not regarded as an 'industry', farming is indeed that, and in Hampshire and the Isle of Wight, as in most rural areas, has always been of paramount importance. The agricultural history of the region has generally reflected the national picture. Farming in Britain dates from at least the Neolithic period, and the work of mainstream archaeologists has provided sufficient evidence to offer an impression of the methods used, and crops cultivated since that time. In some ways, agricultural practice remained unchanged for many centuries: for instance, the metal sickles of the Bronze Age were little different from those wielded by the Victorian farm worker. In Hampshire, an Iron Age farm has been recreated at Butser, near Petersfield, and the pioneering experimental archaeology practised there has enabled a far greater understanding of the farming of the last century before Roman occupation.

Many books on agricultural history have been produced - a selection is included in the bibliography (Appendix 1). However, since most of the structures and features surviving in Hampshire and the Isle of Wight date from the 18th and 19th centuries - the Agricultural Revolution - and later, a summary of the changes which have taken place since c.1750 is most appropriate here. Although the pace of change has often been exaggerated by historians - as Chambers and Mingay point out 'the processes of agricultural change are slow and the time span of their germination and maturity is necessarily long'[1] - the sweeping scope of the changes is indisputable. New breeding techniques, experiments with crop rotation systems, the increased use of fertilisers, and technological innovation all played their parts, together with a more scientific approach to agriculture. Publicists such as Arthur Young helped to spread the knowledge of these developments.

After a long period of agricultural depression following the end of the Napoleonic Wars, the years after Queen Victoria's accession were profitable ones for the British farmer. The industrial revolution, with its consequent growth of towns, resulted in greatly increased demand for agricultural produce. These were years of innovation and investment, known as the period of 'high farming'. The situation was helped by outside circumstances: wars, transport costs and technical problems preventing American and Russian farmers from realising the full potential of their land.[2]

In the 1870s, however, the situation changed. The railroads enabled the American prairies to be opened up and before long, with the advantages of large scale mechanisation, cheap grain was being exported to Britain, thus causing problems for the arable farmer. As Chambers and Mingay point out, 'the future for English agriculture lay in reducing costs and becoming more competitive, and in converting a large proportion of arable land to pasture for dairying and beef production'.[3] Even the production of meat was not, however, without problems from competition: the development of refrigeration techniques resulted in an increase of imported meat from the Antipodes and South America, causing prices to fall sharply. Those farmers who survived and remained reasonably profitable during the so-called 'Great Depression' were those who adapted to changing conditions.

In Hampshire and on the Isle of Wight it is possible, even now, to find examples of most types of agricultural activity: sheep husbandry and beef cattle, dairy farming, and arable crops such as wheat, barley and maize. There are also pockets of more specialised activity: for instance, in the north east of Hampshire hops are still grown, although on a much

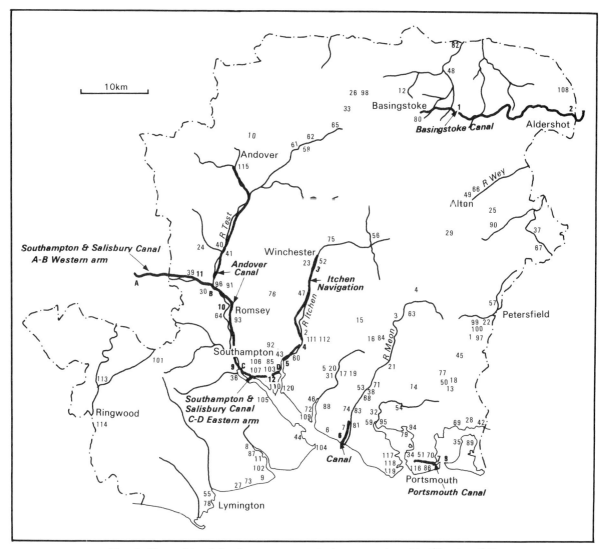

Map 1. Hampshire: inland waterways and places mentioned in Chapters 2–5.

KEY

1. Iron Age Farm Project, Butser
2. Watermeadows, Bishopstoke
3. Watercress beds, Warnford
4. Windpump and farmhouse, Hinton Woodlands Farm
5. Durley Hall Farm – pond, pigsties
6. Brownwich Farm, Titchfield
7. Tithe barn, Titchfield
8. Barn, Beufre Farm, Beaulieu
9. Barn and dovecote, St Leonards Farm, Beaulieu

10. Barn, Parsonage Farm, Hurstbourne Tarrant
11. Barn, cartshed and farmhouse, Keeping Farm, Beaulieu
12. Granary, Stocks Farm, Bramley
13. Granary, Catherington
14. Granary, Rookwood Farm
15. Granary, Woodcote Farm, Upham
16. Granary, Northbrook Farm, Bishops Waltham
17. Botley Farm Museum
18. Stables, Finchdean
19. Stables, Lane End House Farm, Botley

20. Cattlesheds, Snakemoor Farm, Durley
21. Dovecote, St Clairs Farm, Soberton, near Droxford
22. Dovecote, Manor Farm, Langrish
23. Dovecote, Lainston House, Sparsholt
24. Dovecote, Broughton
25. Hopkilns East Worldham
26. Cartshed, Old Burghclere
27. Model Farm, Pylewell
28. Model Farm, Leigh Park
29. Church Farm, Privett
30. Lockerley Hall Farm

31. Farmhouse, Foxholes Farm, Durley
32. Farmhouse, Albany Farm, Fareham
33. Housing, Lower Woodcote Farm, Lichfield
34. Portsmouth Camber
35. Oyster beds, Hayling Island
36. Eling tide mill
37. Headley Mill
38. Chesapeake Mill, Wickham
39. Ford Mill, Lockerley
40. Bossington Mill, Houghton
41. Horsebridge Mill
42. Quay Mill, Emsworth
43. Woodmill, Southampton
44. Ashlett tide mill, Fawley
45. Chalton windmill
46. Bursledon windmill
47. Shawford Mill
48. Sherfield-on-Loddon Mill
49. Maltings, Alton
50. Gales Brewery
51. Whitbread's Brewery, Portsmouth
52. Winchester Brewery
53. Wickham Brewery
54. Southwick Brewhouse
55. Pennington Brewhouse
56. Alresford fulling mill
57. Sheet fulling mill
58. Whitchurch silk mill
59. Ropewalk, Fareham
60. Gaters Mill, Southampton
61. Bere Mill, Whitchurch
62. Paper mill, Laverstoke
63. Papermaker's cottage, Warnford
64. Test Mill, Romsey
65. Town Mill, Overton
66. Kings Mill, Alton
67. Bramshott Paper mill
68. Wickham tannery
69. Havant tannery
70. Copnor tannery

71. Wickham ironworks
72. Bursledon ironworks
73. Sowley ironworks
74. Funtley ironworks
75. Micheldever smithy
76. Hursley smithy
77. Clanfield smithy
78. Salt stores, Pennington
79. Portchester Castle (for Roman bricks)
80. Basing House (brickwork)
81. Place House, Titchfield (brickwork)
82. Bramshill House (brickwork)
83. Funtley brickworks
84. Blanchards works, Bishops Waltham
85. Prudential offices (terracotta), Southampton
86. Prudential offices (terracotta), Portsmouth
87. Baileys Hard brickworks
88. Bursledon brickworks
89. Pycroft's brickworks, Hayling Island
90. Selborne brickworks
91. Michelmersh brickworks
92. Nuffield Theatre, Southampton (brickwork)
93. Courthouse, Romsey (brickwork)
94. Paulsgrove quarry
95. Downend whiting works, Fareham
96. Mottisfont whiting works
97. Limekiln, Butser
98. Limekiln, Old Burghclere
99. Limekiln, Buriton
100. Glassmaking site, Buriton
101. Gunpowder site, Fritham
102. Bucklers Hard
103. Supermarine works site, Southampton
104. Calshot flying boat base
105. Hythe – aircraft manufacture site
106. Imperial House, Southampton
107. Flying boat terminal (H.M.S. *Wessex*)
108. Royal Aircraft Establishment, Farnborough
109. A.V.R.O. Factory, Hamble
110. Woolhouse, Southampton
111. Carriage and wagon works, Eastleigh
112. Locomotive works, Eastleigh
113. Armfields, Stuckton
114. Armfields, Ringwood
115. Taskers, Andover
116. Portsmouth Naval Base
117. Great Magazine, Priddys Hard
118. Royal Clarence Victualling Yard
119. Froude Testing tank, Gosport
120. Woolston Rolling Mills

INLAND WATERWAYS

1. Greywell tunnel, Basingstoke Canal
2. Ash Lock, Basingstoke Canal
3. Catherine Hill Lock, Itchen Navigation
4. Conegar Lock, Itchen Navigation
5. Mansbridge, Itchen Navigation
6. Sea Lock, Titchfield Canal
7. Sea Lock, Portsmouth Canal
8. Engine House, Portsmouth Canal
9. Redbridge, Andover Canal
10. Romsey, Andover Canal
11. Lock No. 4, Western Arm, Southampton & Salisbury Canal
12. Canal tunnel, Eastern Arm, Southampton & Salisbury Canal

reduced scale; on the Isle of Wight their cultivation has ceased. Other Hampshire crops include watercress in the river valleys, and soft fruits, such as strawberries, in the southern part of the county. William Driver, writing towards the end of the 18th century, mentions another feature of Hampshire saying that it is 'particularly famous for water meadows, which are extremely productive, and generally very well-managed'.[4]

It is rare to find water meadows in use today, but their importance in the past was considerable. First recorded as being worked in the late 16th century, they were formed by constructing a series of channels on grassland near to a river, and by means of sluices could effect controlled drowning of surrounding land, thus producing an early grass crop. Until well into the present century, when increased importation of feedstuffs and greater use of artificial fertilisers rendered water meadows redundant, this form of irrigation was widely adopted. The water, usually containing silt which supplied extra nutrients, was of a slightly higher temperature than the static water in winter, since it came from natural reservoirs in the hills. A number of examples of disused watermeadows may be seen in Hampshire, one of the best being at Bishopstoke (SU 465187), where remains of drainage channels and sluices survive, near to Conegar Lock on the Itchen Navigation.

Watercress, a crop still frequently associated with Hampshire, thrives in the specially prepared beds of water from chalk sources. It may be seen growing in many areas of the county, an example being at Warnford, adjacent to the A32 road (SU 621231).

Water supply has always been an important factor in the choice of sites for farmsteads. Only recently have artificial sources of water been available, so the majority of farms have grown up near to a river or spring. In some places wells were dug, and a variety of ways of raising the water were adopted. For instance, wind-driven pumps were sometimes used and, although only a few of these remain in service, many examples of such installations survive, as at Hinton Woodlands Farm (SU 635275), near Bramdean. Wheels, using man or animal power, were also employed, but these will be mentioned in more detail in Chapter 6, in the section on water supply, as similar devices served private houses. Where possible, farmers also constructed ponds to collect available moisture. Of these, some are dug in clay, and so retain water without lining, while others have be to lined. At Durley Hall Farm (SU 522181), examples of both kinds may be seen.

Before the coming of steam power, and other new forms of energy, farmers frequently supplemented man and animal power by the use of water. This was made possible by the fast flowing chalk streams of the county and, in a number of places, water wheels were installed to provide the power to drive farm machinery. Little remains of most of these, although an excavation undertaken by the Southampton University Industrial Archaeology Group in 1981-2, at Brownwich Farm, Titchfield (SU 519037), revealed a former wheel pit, and parts of a wooden waterwheel which drove machinery in the adjacent barn.[5]

Farm Buildings
Barns and Granaries
Both Hampshire and the Isle of Wight have a rich legacy of historic farm buildings, although increasingly these are being converted to alternative uses. A few early structures may still be seen, for example the Tithe Barn at Titchfield (SU 539065) which dates from the 15th century, and has in recent years been restored. However, in many instances barns have either been obliterated, or demolished and rebuilt, and the majority of historic farm buildings in the area date from the 18th and 19th centuries.

For the barns still in agricultural use, a change in function has been inevitable. Once used for threshing and winnowing, the mechanisation of these processes has led to barns being rendered obsolete.[6] Uses now include the storage of fodder for livestock, or other

4. Windpump, Hinton Woodlands Farm, Bramdean.

5. Recovery of pieces of waterwheel, Brownwich Farm.

oddments which the farmer wishes to house. Alternatively, some barns have become garages, or occasionally, and often less successfully, dwellings.

Many fine barns survive, little altered, in Hampshire and the Isle of Wight. Their design varies considerably: walls may be of stone and flint, brick or weatherboarding, or a combination of these, depending on the building materials available locally. A few thatched roofs survive, but more usually roofs are now of tiles, slates or corrugated iron. The number of wagon entrances and bays vary, as does the size of the buildings, and the roof construction can take a number of forms, although the queen post truss is the most common. Many barns are aisled, especially in Hampshire. Consequently, their roof line is low, necessitating porches over the wagon doors, a feature which, although present in places, is not so common on the Isle of Wight.

6. Barn, Beufre Farm, Beaulieu.

The choice for examples of fine barns in the area is considerable. In Hampshire, amongst the most interesting are some in the New Forest area. At Beufre Farm (SU 385012), a brick barn on stone foundations survives in agricultural use. At nearby St. Leonard's Farm, also on the Beaulieu estate (SZ 406982), the barn is a most remarkable structure. Of the original medieval tithe barn, an enormous building, little more than the two gable ends remains. However, a later barn, occupying about a quarter of the original area, makes use of part of the western gable and a wall from the old barn. Use was also made in its construction of materials from the earlier barn. It is altogether a fascinating site: behind the barn, it is just possible to discern the remains of a former horse walk - a rare survival in the area.

As already mentioned, some of the county's finest barns are no longer in farm use. For example, at Parsonage Farm, Hurstbourne Tarrant (SU 384531), the thatched barn, of weatherboarded construction, is put to a variety of social uses: even a wedding reception has been held inside. At Keeping Farm, near Beaulieu (SU 403004), the brick barn with its distinctive air vents and tiled roof is now used as a garage.

The Isle of Wight, too, has some excellent barns. At Chale Farm (SZ 485778), a late medieval structure survives, built of stone in ecclesiastical style; this was almost certainly once a tithe barn. At Cheverton Farm, Apse Heath (SZ 579834), there is an excellent example of a brick barn on a stone base, its roof thatched and supported by queen post trusses. Somewhat unusually, it has a porch on its eastern side, while the western side is plain.

Another farm building which has undergone a change of use is the granary. Once used to store grain, the farmer's most valuable asset, it is often sited near to the farmhouse, but today is normally used for general storage. The design is similar in Hampshire and the Isle of Wight, almost invariably resting on staddle stones. This is a regional feature: many areas of the country have relied on storing grain in buildings above cartsheds or barns.[7] Staddle stones are mushroom-shaped and are intended to make it impossible for vermin to enter the granary.

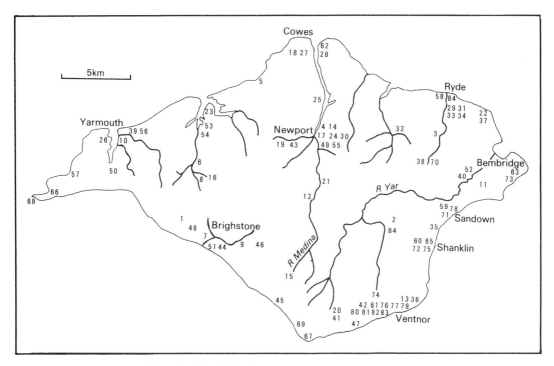

Map 2. Isle of Wight: places mentioned in the text.

KEY

1. Threshing barn, Chale
2. Barn and stables, Cheverton Farm, Apse Heath
3. Granary, Smallbrook Farm
4. Hop kiln, Briddlesford Lodge Farm
5. Cart shed, Rew Street Farm
6. Lower Calborne Mill
7. Brighstone Mill
8. Upper Calborne Mill
9. Yafford Mill
10. Yarmouth tide mill
11. Bembridge windmill
12. Gatcombe mill
13. Burts Brewery, Ventnor
14. Mew Langton's Brewery, Newport
15. 'Star' Brewery, Chale Green
16. Fulling Mill, Calborne
17. Lace Factory, Newport
18. Ropewalk, Cowes
19. Paper Mill, Clatterford
20. Nettlecombe smithy

21. Blackwater smithy
22. Salterns, Seaview
23. Salterns, Newtown
24. Clay pipe manufacture, Newport
25. Cement Works, near Cowes
26. Sandhouse, Yarmouth
27. Arctic Boatyard (Marvins), Cowes
28. Gridiron Shed, Cowes
29. St John's Road railway works, Ryde
30. Gasholder, Newport
31. Gas Company building, Ryde
32. Retort House, Havenstreet
33. Gas lamp, Newport
34. Gas lamp/drinking fountain, Ryde
35. Skew Bridge Electricity works, Lake (site)
36. Electricity works, Ventnor
37. Electric lamp, Seaview
38. Knighton waterworks (site)
39. Pump, Yarmouth

40. Pump, Brading
41. Water standards, Whitwell
42. Ventnor waterworks
43. Donkey wheel, Carisbrooke
44. Milestone, Brighstone
45. Milestone, Blackgang
46. Milestone, Shorwell
47. Tollhouse, St Lawrence
48. Tollhouse, Hulverstone
49. Tollhouse, Newport
50. Tollhouse, Afton
51. Bridge, Grange Chine
52. Brading quay
53. Newtown quay
54. Shalfleet quay
55. Newport quay
56. Yarmouth pier
57. Totland Bay pier
58. Ryde pier
59. Sandown pier
60. Shanklin pier
61. Ventnor pier
62. Cowes floating bridge
63. Hangar, Bembridge
64. Hangar, Apse Heath

65. Hangar, Shanklin
66. Rocket test site, Totland Bay
67. Lighthouse, St Catherine's Point
68. Lighthouse, Needles
69. Salt Pot, St Catherine's Hill
70. Seamark, Ashey Down
71. Post box, Sandown
72. Post box, Shanklin
73. Telephone box, Bembridge
74. Icehouse, Appuldurcombe
75. Shanklin Theatre
76. Ventnor Winter Gardens
77. Ventnor Pavilion
78. Rivoli cinema, Sandown
79. Bandstand, Ventnor
80. Former bathing machine, Ventnor
81. The *Crab and Lobster*, Ventnor
82. The *Hole in the Wall*, Ventnor
83. Hurst's shop, Ventnor
84. Union Street, Ryde

7. Granary at Woodcote Farm, Upham.

8. Granary at Smallbrook Farm, near Ryde, Isle of Wight.

9. Grain bins at the Botley Farm Museum granary.

In the area covered by this book granaries have been constructed of various materials: timber weatherboarding with either vertical or horizontal planking, or timber framing with brick infill. Some retain their original thatch, but many now have tiled, slate or asbestos roof coverings. The majority are single storey, but two storey granaries may be seen, as at Stocks Farm, Bramley (SU 652595). Granaries are fairly common in Hampshire, although many have in recent years been neglected, and dereliction has set in. Amongst interesting examples of these buildings are those at Catherington (SU 693139) and Rookwood Farm, Denmead (SU 653133), both timber-framed structures, with brick infill. Of similar construction, but with the unusual feature of an unglazed window with wooden mullions, is the granary at Woodcote Farm, Upham (SU 545217). That at Northbrook Farm, Bishops Waltham (SU 555181) is weatherboarded with a hipped tiled roof, a common design.

On the Isle of Wight, the granary at Smallbrook Farm, near Ryde (SZ 595907) is also of weatherboarding, but its roof is of slate. It is fairly unusual for the original grain bins to survive in a granary today, but an example may be seen at Botley Farm Museum (SU 508119), a complex of traditional buildings now open to the public, and in the care of the Hampshire County Council Recreation Department.

Animal dwellings
The legacy of housing for livestock is far less rich than that for the storage of crops. Although examples may be found of cattlesheds, stables and pigsties, these are frequently of less solid construction than, for example, barns, and have also often been subjected to radical modernisation. Details of such buildings vary, but the majority in Hampshire and on the Isle of Wight are of brick with roofs of tiles or slates. As is the case with barns and granaries, many of these buildings have witnessed a change of use, or abandonment. This is particularly true in the case of pigsties. Before the Victorian era pigs tended not to have special accommodation; in the 19th century it became customary to build pigsties within the farmstead. In recent times, custom has reversed, with pigs normally being kept out in the fields, where shelter is provided for them. With pigsties being difficult to adapt to other uses, dereliction is common, and many former pigsties have been demolished. Examples do survive, though: at Durley Hall Farm (SU 522181) two purpose-built sets may be seen, one free standing, the other incorporated into the side of a barn - a later addition to a building of 17th-century date.

Stables have, in general, fared better, and many remain in use, as at Finchdean (SU 737126), where four bays of a fine stone and flint building with brick quoins and a slate roof survive. Of similar size, but disused, is the brick stable building at Lane End House Farm, Botley (SU 498162), which bears a date stone of 1898, and is adjacent to what was formerly a coach house. The buildings are now used for general storage. An interesting Isle of Wight example is at Cheverton Farm, Apse Heath (SZ 572834). This is built of brick, with a slate roof, and adjoins the barn.

Examples of cattlesheds often now used as stores may also be found. At Snakemoor Farm, Durley (SU 504163), for instance, a brick building, still retaining its drainage channel, dates from the Victorian era. It would have housed quite a number of beasts, being 120 feet long.

One form of animal housing which is becoming increasingly rare in Hampshire is the dovecote. At one time these were important, since the birds not only provided additional meat and eggs during the winter, but also residues for the dung heap. Once the revolution in agriculture of the 18th and 19th centuries resulted in stock being kept all year in greater numbers, the dovecote's role declined. Furthermore, the birds came to be regarded as more of a nuisance than an asset, because of the damage they inflicted on crops. Now dovecotes are rarely retained for their original purpose, but some survive in other uses. Many are free

10. Pigsties, Durley Hall Farm, Durley.

standing, such as that at St. Clair's Farm, Soberton (SU 605154), a very attractive brick and flint building. At Manor Farm, Langrish (SU 712240), the dovecote has been restored by the Hampshire Buildings Preservation Trust, and is built mainly of stone, with brick quoins. It is much earlier in date than that at St. Clair's Farm, and probably medieval. At St. Leonard's Farm. Beaulieu (SZ 406982), the dovecote forms part of a range of farm buildings around a yard, all constructed of the distinctive local yellow-coloured brick. Dovecotes may also be found on large estates, close to the manor house, as at Lainston House, Sparsholt (SU 444317), and at Broughton a good example exists in the churchyard (SU 309329). This is cylindrical in shape, and has recently undergone restoration. Its role would have been to provide meat and eggs for the church's incumbent and his family.

Hopkilns

In the latter part of the 19th and early 20th centuries the hop was an important crop in north east Hampshire, and was also cultivated on the Isle of Wight. It was sold at local markets; Weyhill Fair is probably the most famous. During this century, although some hops are still grown in the area around Alton, this is of less importance as a cheaper imported product has become more readily available. Furthermore, drying is now usually undertaken by the buyers of the hops, thus rendering the area's hopkilns redundant. Some survive little altered, but increasingly they are converted for alternative uses, in particular as houses. Generally, Hampshire's hopkilns are quite different from the familiar Kentish

11. (*above*) Dovecote, St Clair's Farm, near Droxford.

12. (*right*) Dovecote in Broughton churchyard.

oasts, tending to be pyramidal rather than cylindrical in shape. An interesting set of kilns survive at East Worldham (SU 748382), and these are typical. Of the three, all pyramidal in shape, one is in stone, the others brick. They have been converted dramatically in the last few years, for residential use. On the Isle of Wight, a most interesting pair of kilns, now disused, survive at Briddlesford Lodge Farm (SZ 534902). They are constructed of brick, and are of a very unusual design.

Cartsheds

These, too, have tended to be adapted to suit changing agricultural needs, now used for tractors, or even motor cars, rather than traditional carts and wagons. They have a poorer survival rate in Hampshire and on the Isle of Wight than in many counties. One factor which may have contributed to this is the local mode of construction, using wooden rather than stone posts to support the roof. Examples do, however, survive, for instance at Keeping Farm, Beaulieu (SU 403004), now used as a wood store, and at Old Burghclere (SU 469578). As a rule, major conversions of cartsheds do not occur, although a striking exception to this may be seen on the Isle of Wight. At Rew Street (SZ 471943), a four-bay stone cartshed of traditional design, bearing the date 1807, was until several years ago unaltered. The author photographed it in the autumn of 1983, when it was being used to give shelter to a motor car. A visit to the site in the spring of 1985 revealed a total transformation, the cartshed having undergone conversion to a dwelling. The inscribed date survived, however.

Model Farms

These are complexes of considerable historical interest mainly dating from the mid-Victorian period, when capital for investment was plentiful. In Hampshire they are usually linked to great estates and the intention was to produce a purpose-built farmstead combining the best possible design of buildings, with the latest innovations in agricultural practice.

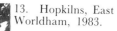
13. Hopkilns, East Worldham, 1983.

14. Hopkilns, East Worldham, 1987.

15. Hopkilns, Briddlesford Lodge Farm, Isle of Wight.

Whereas most farmsteads have evolved over centuries, 'model farms' were built as one unit, often including accommodation for the farmer and his workers. A number survive, four examples being Pylewell Home Farm (SZ 358960) in the New Forest; Leigh Park Estate Farm (SU 722084), which was owned by Sir Thomas Staunton from 1828 until 1858;[8] Church Farm, Privett (SU 675268), and Lockerley Hall Farm (SU 293280).

Church Farm was part of the Nicholson estate, and dates from the 1870s, being contemporary with other local buildings, such as the church, paid for by the Nicholsons. The buildings are all matching, of brick and flint, and form a most attractive complex. Besides a cartshed, and cattle accommodation arranged around a yard, there is a farmhouse and estate cottages, in the same style. The farm is still a working unit.

Lockerley Hall Farm, however, is no longer operational. It is, nevertheless, a collection of buildings of outstanding interest. The former cattlesheds, of brick, retain their stalls of cast iron, complete with the crest of the Dalgety family, for whom the farm was built in the 1860s. It is worth noting that these date, not surprisingly, from the age of 'high farming' when money for investment was freely available. At Lockerley, the estate buildings include stables, a smoking house and a blacksmith's shop. Without doubt, though, the most impressive building is the polygonal dairy, marble lined and with its fountain intact.

Farm Accommodation
Having described examples of the buildings which housed crops and animals, it is perhaps appropriate also to mention the dwellings erected for the farmer and his employees. Many fine farmhouses may be seen, such as Foxholes Farm, Durley (SU 491172), which dates in part from the 17th century, with later additions. The farmhouse at Hinton Woodlands Farm, Bramdean (SU 635275), is an impressive structure, with the unusual feature of shutters on the front door, whilst at Albany Farm, Fareham (SU 578090), the red brick house adjoins the farmstead, although set slightly apart. At Keeping Farm, Beaulieu, too, the house is very attractive, and this farmstead is an excellent example of farm buildings being re-used for non-agricultural purposes.

Once the custom of 'living in' for workers ended, many tied cottages were provided for farmworkers. Although some of these were little more than hovels, and have long since disappeared, many were solid dwellings and are frequently still occupied by farmworkers. They often complement the design of the farmhouse, as at Church Farm, Privett. At Lower Woodcote Farm, near Litchfield (another Nicholson farm), a pair of such cottages survives (SU 444548), dating from the 18th century, standing to the north of the farmhouse. In 1919, a further three cottages (SU 445546) were built to the south of the farmhouse, in a quite different style.[9]

As already suggested, agricultural practice had to adapt to changing conditions in the last quarter of the 19th century. As cheap foreign grain and meat became available, many farmers changed to market gardening, dairy farming and the production of soft fruits such as strawberries. Increase in local demand was one advantage but, more importantly, the coming of the railways meant that produce from Hampshire farms could be speedily conveyed to London, and thus the county's agriculture managed to remain reasonably profitable. Today, far fewer workers are required as the industry becomes more technologically based, a contrast to the labour intensive structure of the past. Nevertheless, farming remains a vital part of the area's economy.

Fishing
Although fishing has traditionally had a role in the economic life of Hampshire and the Isle of Wight, it has tended to be on a much smaller scale than in other areas, and has left little evidence to be seen today. At such places as Portsmouth Camber (SZ 630995), fishing

16. Church Farm, Privett.

17. Dairy at Lockerley Hall Farm, Lockerley.

boats may be seen, but the only area which has left a tangible legacy is the cultivation of oyster beds. In the south-east corner of Hampshire, particularly at Emsworth and Hayling Island, this was once an important local industry. In the late 19th century, oyster beds were enclosed by an embankment (originally built in connection with a railway) on the north west coast of Hayling Island (SU 716038). These beds remained in use until the 1920s, and have recently been rebuilt and are once more in production.[10] Emsworth's oyster industry suffered a mortal blow when, in 1902, three people died after eating oysters at a banquet in Winchester - the result of untreated sewage polluting the beds.[11]

Chapter Three

Industries based on the Products of Agriculture

A considerable amount of economic activity depends on the products of agriculture for raw materials: grain for flour milling, barley and hops for brewing. Textile production – woollen and silk manufacture, and rope making – needs products which are in one way or another derived from farming. Even paper making, once a very important Hampshire industry, used rags as a raw material, and the production of leather by tanning depends on animal skins and tree bark.

Flour Milling

Man has ground grain to provide flour for many centuries, at least from biblical times. The earliest crushing was done by man and animal power, at first by pounding between stones, and then with the quern, the forerunner of the watermill and the windmill. Thus was the principle established of a stone base, with the grain being placed between this and another stone which was moved, at first, backwards and forwards. The next development was the rotary quern, the top stone revolving on a central pivot, albeit somewhat irregularly.

The first reference to what John Reynolds describes as 'man's earliest engines'[1] dates from c.85 B.C., when mention is made by the poet Antipate of Thessalonica of a watermill. Within a few decades, these are also recorded as being in use in China, and it is likely that they were introduced to the western world, too, at about this time. These were, however, horizontal mills, but it was in the Roman period that the vertical mill, from which today's watermills developed, first appeared. Both types of mill were at one time in use in Britain, although it appears that in the southern counties only the vertical mill was adopted.

As in the case of the watermill, the origins of the use of windpower for grinding corn are not entirely clear. Certainly the principle of the windmill was known in Persia (Iran) in the 10th century,[2] but how long it had been in use is uncertain. These mills were similar mechanically to the horizontal watermills. It seems likely, however, that the origins of what we recognise as a windmill are to be found in Europe. The earliest documentary evidence relating to the existence of a postmill in Britain dates from the late 12th century, when mention is made of such a structure at Weedley in Yorkshire.[3]

Over the centuries, both windmill and watermill technology increased in sophistication, but the basic principle remained unchanged. Many of today's watermills stand on sites which were occupied by a mill at the time of the Domesday survey, 900 years ago, although in Hampshire and the Isle of Wight, as in other areas, these are now in stone or brick, more durable than their wooden predecessors. The area is one in which the watermill has inevitably predominated, with reliable fast-flowing streams to provide the power. One should remember, nevertheless, that windmills did operate in Hampshire and the Isle of Wight, and the balance in favour of waterpower is not so substantial as was once believed. This impression resulted in reliance purely on archaeology (watermills have a far higher survival rate that windmills), and the work done by Dr. Derek Moore, using documentary evidence on Hampshire windmill sites, has helped to redress the balance.

Until the transport revolution, the local mill played a vital role in every community. Providing the main ingredient for man's daily bread ensured that the miller was an important figure. Over the centuries both he and his mills have appeared in many illustrations, such as the early 14th-century Luttrell Psalter, where a watermill, complete with overshot wheel, and an eel trap (a useful sideline for many a miller), can be seen. Similarly, in the cloisters of Norwich Cathedral one of the bosses includes a carving of a windmill, typical of East Anglia where wind-power predominates.

Farmers bringing their grain to the miller in early times paid for his services often in kind rather than cash, and a fixed amount of the flour produced would be available for the miller to sell. Gradually the payment of the toll in money became more common, until 1796 when a statute made this compulsory.[4]

Most of the mills which survive in Hampshire and on the Isle of Wight date from the 18th and 19th centuries. When Southampton University Industrial Archaeology Group undertook a survey in 1978, 200 mill sites were identified in Hampshire and 29 on the Isle of Wight.[5] Of these, about one third had been demolished, leaving archaeological evidence, such as watercourses or sluices, and one third had been converted to alternative uses. Of the remainder, a handful were still in operation; the rest lay disused.

The decline of the small mill was due to many separate factors. Probably the most significant was the availability of large quantities of cheap grain from North America, once the mechanisation of agriculture had permitted the development of the prairies and improvements in transport had facilitated the export of grain. As already mentioned in the previous chapter, arable farming in Britain declined in importance, and those farmers who remained prosperous did so by making the transition to market gardening and milk production. Large steam-powered roller mills were erected at ports, and such competition naturally had an adverse effect on the small mill. Furthermore roller mills could produce the finer flour for the white bread which became popular at that time, and the installation of such equipment was usually too expensive for a small mill. Mills are very costly to maintain, both in terms of the maintenance of machinery, and in keeping water channels free from weeds, silt and other obstructions. Although some mills installed water turbines, or adopted other power sources, such as steam, gas or electricity in order to improve efficiency, the small mill was doomed. The watermills also had to contend with the increased abstraction of water from rivers as demand, both for industrial use and for domestic consumption, increased.

At the turn of the century, evidence gathered from trade directories suggests that the number of working watermills in Hampshire had dropped to 98, with 22 on the Isle of Wight. By the beginning of the Second World War, these figures were 34 and 11 respectively.[6] Now the number in commercial use can be counted on the fingers of one hand.

Mills in Hampshire and the Isle of Wight are generally of brick or stone; the only windmills of which remains survive are tower mills. Although at one time the area was rich in tide mills, only that at Eling (SU 365125), restored in the late 1970s, is in operation and producing flour. Tide mills are identical to other watermills in every respect bar one: instead of relying on a river or stream, they are fed, wholly or partially, by the tide. This gives them the advantage of being able to mill for a set period each day, with no fear of water shortage; on the other hand the miller would be subject to very unsocial hours of work. In Hampshire, the only watermill producing stone ground flour in quantity, apart from Eling Tide Mill, is Headley Mill (SU 813355). There has been a mill on this site for many centuries, the present building being a fine continuous range of mill and mill house, built of stone. Water from the River Wey feeds into the mill pond, providing the power to turn the $12\frac{1}{2}$ foot diameter iron waterwheel.

Animal feed is still prepared at Chesapeake Mill, Wickham (SU 574116), with much of the work now being done by electricity, although the water turbine is still used for certain tasks. The mill has a fascinating history, dating from 1820, when it was built with some of the timbers from the American frigate *Chesapeake*, captured by the British in 1813 and later broken up.

18. Headley Mill, near Bordon.

19. Chesapeake Mill, Wickham.

20. Horsebridge Mill, near Romsey.

21. Ashlett Mill, Fawley.

On the Isle of Wight flour is still produced commercially at Lower Calbourne Mill (SZ 414878), and animal feed at Brighstone Mill (SZ 425823). Two island watermills are open to the public: Upper Mill, Calbourne (SZ 414868) and Yafford (SZ 446822), and afford the chance of viewing mill machinery.

A number of excellent books have been published explaining fully the technological development of both wind and watermills, and some of them are listed in the bibliography.

Many mill buildings have been re-used for other purposes. This has contributed to the survival of a far greater number of watermills than windmills. Many have been converted to dwellings, more or less sympathetically, and particularly good examples may be seen at Lockerley (Ford Mill, SU 296270) and Houghton (Bossington Mill, SU 340313) in Hampshire, and on the Isle of Wight at Yarmouth Tide Mill (SZ 356091).

There are many other uses for redundant watermills. Horsebridge Mill (SU 346305) is now in use for light engineering work, while Quay Mill, Emsworth (SU 748055), is now a sailing club. Numerous recreational activities have been housed in former mills: Woodmill, Southampton (SU 439152) is a canoeing centre, and Ashlett Tide Mill, near Fawley (SU 466032), accommodates a social club.

The re-use of windmills is far less successful. Their shape does not make them ideal for conversion to dwellings, although some, such as that at Chalton (SU 716162), have been so adapted.

Only one windmill surviving in Hampshire is complete enough for restoration to be possible, and indeed, this is almost finished. Bursledon Windmill (SU 482108), which has a remarkable history, was rescued from dereliction by the Hampshire Buildings Preservation Trust. Work has been undertaken to restore both mill and machinery, and it is hoped that, before very long, flour will once more be ground there. On the Isle of Wight, Bembridge Windmill (SZ 640875), owned by the National Trust and open to the public, is virtually complete although not in working order.

Unless new functions are found for them, many disused mills will crumble. In Hampshire, mills like that at Shawford (SU 474250) and at Sherfield-on-Loddon (SU 683582) cause concern, and on the Isle of Wight the picturesque and unusual mill at Gatcombe (SZ 498852) is deteriorating and may not survive. The Hampshire Mills Group was formed some years ago with the object of trying to retain as many local mills as possible, either as working units or, if necessary, by conversion, and to offer help and advice to mill owners. (See Appendix 3.)

Brewing

Like the grinding of corn for flour, the use of processed barley in the manufacture of a beverage has a very long history. Stone reliefs from Egypt survive from about the third century B.C. which show the brewing process.[7] Malting and fermentation were understood, although the product was somewhat crude, and bore little resemblance to the beer drunk today. It was cloudy, and in some instances so thick with unfiltered barley husks that a straw of hollow reed was necessary. The drink was ale, and no hops were used in its manufacture.

Brewing methods gradually became more sophisticated, and in the 15th century hops were introduced into ale,[8] resulting in a drink rather nearer to modern beer. Ale was one of the earliest commodities to be taxed, duty being payable in some way since 1188, when King Henry II introduced the first national tariff on it.

Until the mid-19th century, brewing was generally a localised industry. At first it was done in the home, often by women, and the only places to brew on a large scale were monasteries. Later, inns became more important, brewing their own ales for sale. London, by the end of the 18th century, saw the growth of larger breweries, but it was not until there

22. Bursledon Windmill under restoration in 1983.

23. Bembridge Windmill, Isle of Wight.

24. Gatcombe Mill, Isle of Wight.

were improvements in transport that large-scale production was possible in the provinces. The bulk of the finished product made distribution difficult before the coming of the railways, and every town and many villages had their own brewery.

Once transportation was no longer a problem, large breweries grew larger, and the smaller ones declined. In Hampshire, at the turn of the century, there were more than 80 breweries in operation; by the beginning of the Second World War this was reduced to fifteen.[9] There are now only two major breweries in Hampshire and one on the Isle of Wight, though recent trends have encouraged the resurgence of small domestic breweries.

Malting (the transformation of barley into malt, the basic raw material for beer) has never been an important industry in its own right in Hampshire, as it was, for example, in East Anglia. Some of the larger establishments did at one time, however, have their own maltings, but all the surviving buildings have been converted to other uses. For example, though virtually all the site of Crowley's (later Watney's) brewery at Alton (SU 718391) has been cleared, the former maltings remain in use as a social club. Alton was once an important brewing centre, and one of the two breweries still working in Hampshire, Bass Charrington, can be found there, although this is a modern installation, not a traditional brewery. It is not surprising that brewing should flourish in Alton, the area of the county where both barley and hops were available locally.

One traditional brewery, however, does survive in Hampshire: Gales of Horndean. This has, surprisingly, remained as an independent family firm. Although some modernisation has been necessary, the fine brewhouse tower of 1869 remains, together with a considerable amount of historic machinery (SU 707133). On the Isle of Wight, too, one working brewery of the traditional type remains: Burts of Ventnor (SZ 567777), which has for many years been in the ownership of the Phillips family. Much of the brewery was rebuilt after wartime bomb damage, but beer is produced in much the same way as a century ago.

Modern power sources have, of course, been adopted by most brewers. Until the coming of the steam engine, such tasks as 'mashing' (mixing the malt with water, or 'liquor' as it is always known in a brewery), were done by hand; now electric power is used for brewing apparatus.

Although many fine brewery buildings have been lost – Mew Langton's premises in Newport, Isle of Wight; Coopers in Southampton; Hall's, and Crowley's in Alton; Hyde Abbey Brewery in Winchester – a number survive in alternative use. Whitbreads (formerly Brickwood's) ceased brewing in 1983 in Portsmouth, but the remarkable collection of buildings survive (SU 632005). The complex is fascinating architecturally, having developed over many years and, as it expanded, absorbed a number of structures including houses and a Methodist chapel. Other survivals include Winchester Brewery (SU 480300), now used for storage and distribution, and Wickham Brewery (SU 575116), now offices and housing.

As already mentioned, domestic brewhouses were once common, and in Hampshire, unusually, an example survives in full working order. This is the Golden Lion Brewhouse, Southwick (SU 627085), which served just one public house, with limited off sales, until 1956. Owned by Southwick Estates, it remained disused, despite abortive attempts at restoration, until the late 1970s. In collaboration with the Hampshire Buildings Preservation Trust, the Estate then restored the fabric of the building and, in 1983, Southampton University Industrial Archaeology Group began the task of refurbishing the interior and the machinery, including a single cylinder horizontal steam engine. Work was completed in 1985, and in June of that year a Commemorative Brew was undertaken, and Lord (Asa) Briggs bravely sampled the first pint, to declare the brewery open as a museum. It is now open by appointment: see Appendix 2. Other brewhouse buildings survive, for example at

25. Interior of Southwick Brewhouse.

26. The late Mike Inge working on the restoration of a steam engine at Southwick Brewhouse.

Pennington (SZ 315952), and at Chale Green (SZ 482802) on the Isle of Wight, but these contain little or no machinery.

Textile Manufacture

Many areas of Britain are particularly associated with various types of textile manufacturing activity, though Hampshire and the Isle of Wight have never been among them. Even in the early 18th century, Defoe noted that except for 'a little drugget and shalloon making', nowhere in Hampshire was anyone 'employ'd in any considerable woollen manufacture'.[10] Fairly small scale production of woollen cloth, nevertheless, took place for centuries, and a number of buildings associated with it survive, although all are now used for other purposes.

Most of the remaining woollen production buildings in the area today are related to fulling: cleansing the cloth, followed by pounding it with hammers while it is soaking in a trough of water containing a clay product known as fuller's earth. This matts together the fibres and promotes the maximum amount of felting and shrinking. None of Hampshire's former fulling mills contain any machinery, but buildings may be seen, for example at Alresford (SU 585332), a thatched timber-framed structure with brick infill, now colour washed, and at Sheet (SU 761241), where the mid-18th century building bears a datestone and a fire insurance plaque. Both are now residences. On the Isle of Wight at Fulling Mill Farm, Calbourne (SZ 419869) only the name and a few minor earthworks identify the site.[11]

The British silk industry dates from the latter part of the 17th century, the years following the Civil War when Protestant emigrés sought refuge in England, bringing with them their various skills. Some buildings associated with silk manufacture at this time survive in Winchester, but more remarkable is Whitchurch Silk Mill (SU 462478), arguably the finest industrial building in Hampshire, dating from c.1800. Built of thick chalk blocks, covered by a skin of red brick, it was initially used for the handweaving of wool, and for stay-making. By the 1830s, it had become a silk mill, and is still in use today, producing silk for the legal and academic market. In 1985 it was threatened with closure, but its purchase by the Hampshire Buildings Preservation Trust has secured its future. Although electric power is now used, the mill's waterwheel was recently restored, and among the looms are some dating from the latter part of the 19th century.

On the Isle of Wight, in Newport, is another fine building once associated with textile manufacture. Constructed of attractive yellow brick, the former lace factory of Messrs. Nunn and Co. (SZ 504895) dates from the mid-1820s. In 1833, this company took out a patent to make the very fine French Blond lace. Trading ceased, however, about 1875, and the building is now used as offices for a government department.

Rope Making

In any area where maritime activities flourish, rope manufacture is usually prominent. For many centuries rope was made, using imported hemp, by traditional methods in distinctive long, narrow buildings where the yarn was stretched between revolving hooks which twisted it together. Although this method may still be seen at Chatham Dockyard, all the ropewalks of Hampshire and the Isle of Wight are now either disused or re-used for other purposes. The best example is without doubt that in Portsmouth Dockyard (see Chapter 5), but other examples survive. These are, not surprisingly, to be found near former shipyards. For instance, near Lower Quay, Fareham, is an old ropewalk (SU 577055) which has a most interesting history. In recent years the building has been used for light industry, but in the Napoleonic Wars it was a prison hospital, and in the 17th century, when Fareham was used as a refuge for ships of the Royal Navy, it was for a time a hospital for sick and wounded seamen. Only the shell of the ropewalk survives, and it is apparent that even this has

27. Loom at Whitchurch Silk Mill.

28. Winding at Whitchurch Silk Mill.

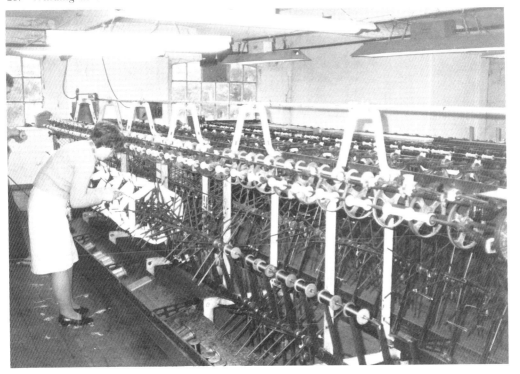

29.   Ropewalk, Fareham.

undergone quite considerable structural alteration. On the Isle of Wight, a building once used as a ropewalk survives in West Cowes (SZ 498955).

Paper Manufacture

Despite records of paper being made in China as early as A.D.105, the process did not reach England until the last years of the 15th century. The technique of paper making by the hand or vat method had gradually spread west, via the Middle East, to Europe. The principal raw materials were textiles: fine linen for good quality white paper, and rags and coarser material for poorer quality brown paper such as for wrapping. An important factor was water supply, both for use in the manufacturing process and to provide power. The traditional method of making paper is described by A.H. Shorter in his *Water Paper-Mills in England* (see Appendix 1), and was little changed for centuries. As Dr. Thomas points out in his article 'Hampshire and the Company of White Paper Makers',[12] the county has long been associated with the production of writing materials. In the 13th century, parchment was being made at Andover, and it is possible that this ancient craft may have been carried out in Havant, well known for its parchment industry, from an even earlier date.[13]

It is not difficult to suggest why parchment and paper were both important industries in Hampshire. The county's chalk streams, pure and reliable, ensured that the mills generally enjoyed a steady and suitable supply of water. Problems did arise on occasion: production had to be cut back if temperatures dropped sufficiently for water to freeze. Shortage of materials was not uncommon, and in 1700 it was considered usual in the industry for the working year to be limited to about 200 days.[14]

Most of Hampshire's mills produced brown paper, with the exception of the mills at South Stoneham, near Southampton, and a few others. At South Stoneham, the River Itchen provided water power for the mills operated by the Company of White Paper Makers.[15] This was a company, formed in 1686, many of whose members were French Protestant refugees. As in the case of silk manufacture, the influx of Huguenots in the 17th century had a marked influence on the development of the British paper industry.[16] The site, formerly known as Up Mills, now houses Gaters Mill (SU 455156), and is used for light industry. The buildings which survive are primarily 19th century, but may well have been used for paper manufacture which continued until c.1865. A map of 1825 shows two mills on the site, one producing flour and one paper.[17]

It was at this mill that, in the early 18th century, Henri de Portal, a Huguenot refugee, was apprenticed to learn the art of paper making.[18] Thus began a career which helped to establish Hampshire as an important centre of the industry. In 1712 and 1719 Portal set up his own paper mills, the first at Bere Mill, Whitchurch (SU 478481), the other at nearby Laverstoke (SU 492487). In 1724, he was awarded the contract for the manufacture of Bank of England note paper, a franchise held by the Portals ever since. Bere Mill later became a corn mill, and is now a residence, but the Laverstoke site, together with the premises at Overton, has continued to be associated with the manufacture of paper.

30. Bere Mill, Whitchurch

An early Hampshire paper mill was that at Warnford. It was built c.1618 by the then lord of the manor, Sir Thomas Neale. Although only a small production unit, Warnford

Paper Mill operated for at least 170 years, but it had ceased production by 1816.[19] As the years passed the building steadily became more derelict, and in the early 1950s what remained of the wooden structure was destroyed in a storm. A by-pass sluice and the papermaker's cottage (SU 621221) however, can be seen.

A number of former paper mills can be seen in Hampshire, all in other uses. Test Mill, Romsey (SU 348215) began life as a fulling mill, but from 1773 until the First World War produced paper. It is now used for industry and also houses a trout farm. Town Mill, Overton (SU 516498), now under conversion, was once part of the Portal empire, being used for preparing rags for use at Laverstoke. Kings Mill, Alton (SU 723396) produced handmade paper from 1759 until 1909. Now used by a packaging company, by 1865 Kings Mill was mainly using steam rather than water power, and provided employment for more than a hundred people.[20] A final example is Bramshott Mill (SU 819345), which was in use from 1684 until 1926. The mill's history is well documented, and it was rebuilt in 1856 following a fire. Extended in 1876, it was taken over by Portals in 1907, and made paper for postal orders until its closure. Most of the buildings survive in industrial use.[21]

31. Paper mill, Bramshott.

The employment of children was commonplace in Hampshire's paper-making industry. For instance, at John Gater's mill, in 1845, three girls and two boys are recorded as working at hot-pressing handmade paper. It is interesting to note that the girls were paid by the piece, and their earnings averaged 6d. per day, while the boys were paid by the day, receiving about 8d.[22]

In the 18th century, paper was also made on the Isle of Wight, but here there is little surviving archaeological evidence. Kenneth Major mentions Clatterford Mill, Carisbrooke (SZ 482875), which produced paper during the first half of the 18th century;[23] now only a leat remains to remind us of its existence.

Like so many of the industries described in this book, paper making was once important in the area; it survives at a single location, but unlike other crafts has left relatively little evidence of its golden past.

Tanning

As with paper making, tanning was at one time a very important occupation in Hampshire, but little archaeological evidence remains. In recent years, tanneries at Fareham and Portsmouth have been demolished, having been disused for many years. Titchfield tannery, too, was lost in 1983, and new factory units now occupy the site. The roof structure of this building was of special interest, as it seems likely that the decorative iron supports were probably from Funtley ironworks (see Chapter 4).

Some tannery buildings, however, survive in alternative use. One possible example, although evidence concerning it is inconclusive, is at Wickham (SU 574115), opposite Chesapeake Mill. A substantial brick structure, it stands on the bank of the River Meon, a ready water supply being, of course, essential to the transformation of animal skins into leather. There are, however, surviving tannery buildings at Havant (SU 710062), now used as a store by the Portsmouth Water Company, and at Copnor (SU 660013).[24]

Chapter Four

Industries based on Mineral Products

One of the factors which has fostered the impression of Hampshire and the Isle of Wight as an area without much industry – a rural backwater – is the general lack of activities concerned with mineral products. There is, and has been, no coal mining, and virtually no extraction of metalliferous material, although some iron ore deposits exist in the extreme west of Hampshire. Stone quarrying was formerly very important on the Isle of Wight, but this declined after brick became more popular as a building material. Remains of quarrying can be seen, but many sites have been in-filled. There are, however, a number of industries connected with minerals still to be found in the region, and signs of others, once important, but no longer practised.

Although only small quantities of iron ore exist in Hampshire, iron has been worked over the centuries at a number of places, and a few smithies are still working today. Heavy engineering has not been included in this section; it will be dealt with in Chapter 5.

Salt manufacture was once an important part of the economic life of both Hampshire and the Isle of Wight. Brickmaking, too, was significant, and is still carried on at three places in Hampshire. The cement industry still operates on the Isle of Wight, and the remains of limekilns testify to the burning of chalk to produce lime. Other industrial activity covered in this chapter includes the manufacture of gunpowder and glass, and clay pipe making.

Iron Production and Processing
Although it is now known that Hampshire's iron ore deposits are greater than was previously believed, they were still relatively insignificant. The metalliferous ore was found mainly at Hordle and Hengistbury Head, in the extreme south west of the county. Much research remains to be done on ironmaking sites locally, but a number have been identified. Some have very little archaeological remains, but have been traced by the use of documents. For instance, north of Wickham (SU 579126), there was a 17th-century plate mill owned by the Earl of Southampton, and leased to Sir William Uvedale. A map of 1720 shows the works[1] but, since the site has been flooded, the fragments of remaining brickwork can no longer be seen.

Another ironworks site was that at Bursledon (SU 480095), and this, too, has been mainly identified by documents. A map from the 1720s shows 'Mr. Gringoe's furnice'.[2] The Gringoes were a family of ironmasters active in Hampshire during the 17th and 18th centuries. Like so many of their trade they were Quakers, and not only ran the Bursledon works, but also had interests at Sowley and Funtley, and owned land in other areas. A careful investigation of the Bursledon site reveals the outline of the hammer pond, now filled in, but it is a site requiring far more investigation.

At Sowley (SZ 378966), there is one major survival: the pond. A great deal of documentary research has been done for this site,[3] but no major excavation has taken place, which might well reveal remains of the blast furnace which smelted iron from about 1600 to 1750. Work in the associated forge continued from the end of the 17th century for about a hundred years, and activity briefly resumed during the Napoleonic Wars. Final closure came in 1822. This was an important site: its customers included the Board of Ordnance and the East India Company.

Without doubt, the most historically important Hampshire ironworks site was that at

Funtley (SU 550082). From the early 17th century, the Earl of Southampton operated the works; it later passed into the hands of the Gringoe family. Its period of greatest significance dates, however, from the mid-1770s, when Henry Cort, a navy agent, inherited control of the ironworks.[4] He processed iron, mainly scrap, into such items as masthoops for the Admiralty. Cort made major changes, and even contemplated installing a steam engine, consulting Matthew Boulton of Boulton and Watt on the possibility.[5] Although this correspondence is most useful in providing a description of the ironworks at this time, there is no evidence to suggest that steam power was ever adopted. The importance of Funtley is in the experiments which Cort undertook there, which resulted in patents of 1783 and 1784 for rolling and puddling processes. These revolutionised the production of wrought iron: within a decade, Britain changed from an im-

32. Plaque at Funtley ironworks.

porter of the product to a major exporter. Previously British wrought iron had been regarded as of poor quality, and was expensive to make. This was an event of incalculable importance at a time when, within a few years, war with France would make imports very difficult and greatly increase the demand for large quantities of wrought iron. It may even have changed the course of history. The story of Henry Cort is a sad but fascinating one;[6] of his works there are scant remains. Most of the buildings were destroyed in a fire towards the end of the 19th century,[7] but the wheelpit survives, together with some portions of wall, including a bricked-up water channel. The pond, although filled in, is also clearly defined, the banks being of iron slag.[8] The importance of Cort's achievements was finally recognised in 1983, when the Historical Metallurgy Society placed a commemorative plaque on the site, to record the first of Cort's patents two centuries before.

Smithies

A hundred years ago, smithies were a common sight in every town and village, the blacksmith's services being very much in demand, especially for the shoeing of horses. These buildings are becoming increasingly disused, and either demolished or converted. In Hampshire and on the Isle of Wight, smithy buildings survive, and a few are still working, One of the best examples is at Micheldever (SU 514390), where an 18th-century single-storey brick building, with a tiled roof, is still in regular use. At Hursley (SU 428253), however, the smithy ceased to work several years ago, and after a period of disuse is now an antiques shop. One of the most recent examples to go out of use is that at Clanfield (SU 698169). On the Isle of Wight, as on the mainland, smithy buildings can still be seen, for instance at Nettlecombe (SZ 525783) and at Blackwater (SZ 506862).

Salt manufacture

The production of salt in Hampshire and the Isle of Wight, until the discovery of rock salt, and indeed for some time afterwards, was an important local industry. Documentary evidence begins with the Domesday Book, which records that in 1086 Hampshire had 22 saltpans,[9] indicating that the industry was already well established. Of most of the former

33. Micheldever Smithy.

34. Hursley Smithy.

35. Nettlecombe Smithy, Isle of Wight.

salt pans no archaeological evidence remains, although clues can sometimes be found in local references in street or district names to 'salterns'.

Despite the imposition of a salt tax in 1694, and the discovery of rock salt in the same decade, it was many years before the industry in this area was seriously affected, probably because transport difficulties favoured local production of commodities. The beginning of the 19th century, however, witnessed the start of the decline which was to lead to the end of salt production in Hampshire and on the island. The salt tax had been raised dramatically during the Napoleonic Wars and, with more satisfactory transport arrangements, salt extraction by solar evaporation could not compete with the industry in the north of England where rock salt was to be found. At the start of the century, the salt trade of Lymington was second only to that of Liverpool (rock salt came primarily from Cheshire), the comparative figures being 149,839 bushels and 165,985 bushels. By 1815, the returns told a very different story, with Lymington producing 39,365 bushels, against Liverpool's 1,389,199 bushels.[10]

By the latter part of the 19th century, virtually all local saltpans had fallen into disuse, and surviving reminders of this once thriving industry are now scanty. Beside Lower Woodside Creek, near Lymington, which Defoe described as a town 'chiefly noted for making fine salt, which is indeed excellent good',[11] three brick buildings associated with the salt industry may be seen (SZ 326934). Adjacent is the channel where barges brought coal in, and took salt out. On the Isle of Wight, Saltern Cottages, Seaview (SZ 625917) housed workers employed in salt production in the early years of the 19th century. At Newtown (SZ 423913), it is still possible to see the embankments of the collecting ponds and evaporating pans around the creek.

Clay-based industries: Brickmaking
Although brickmaking is no longer practised at all on the Isle of Wight, and only on a relatively small scale in Hampshire, local bricks in the past have been used in buildings all over the world. The area's geological make-up is such that deposited clays and brickearths are plentiful right across the region.

Brickmaking was introduced to England by the Romans, though the techniques were known in other parts of the world from a much earlier date.[12]. Roman bricks were very different in shape from their modern counterparts, being more like thick floor tiles, about 18 inches long and $2\frac{1}{2}$ inches thick.[13]. These survive at a number of locations, including the walls of Portchester Castle (SU 625045).

After the Roman occupation, bricks were not made in England for some centuries, although a number of Saxon and Norman buildings re-used Roman bricks. The earliest certain evidence of the re-introduction of brickmaking in this country dates from the 12th century, in East Anglia. This location is not surprising because of the proximity of Europe, a lack of building stone, and good, suitable clays.[14]

Bricks were imported from the Netherlands into Southampton in the medieval period; these, like Roman bricks, were small in size. The art of brickmaking seems to have revived in Hampshire by the 15th century, with a surviving example in the gateway of Basing House (SU 663526). There is 16th-century brickwork at Place House, Titchfield (SU 543066).

By the 17th century, brick was a popular building material and the Great Fire of London in 1666 stimulated the industry further, since it was realised that timber buildings were very vulnerable to such disasters. One of the finest examples of brickwork from this period, in Hampshire, is Bramshill House, near Hartley Wintney, now a Police Training College (SU 759598). This was built by Lord Zouch between 1605 and 1612, and is one of the county's outstanding buildings.

The 18th century, and in particular the industrial and transport revolutions, provided great impetus for brickmaking. Demand increased for use in houses, factories and public buildings. In 1784, brick tax was levied for the first time, in order to assist the financing of the American War of Independence. This was set first at 2s.6d. per thousand bricks, but the rate varied considerably between that date and 1850 when the tax was abolished.[15] Brick tax initially resulted in an increase in the use of large bricks (such as the Wilkes 'Gobs' still to be seen at Measham in Leicestershire), and in tile-hung walls. The government, however, did not allow this to continue and tax rates were amended accordingly.

The Victorian period saw a dramatic rise in the use and production of bricks. The development of the railway system at first increased demand, as stations, tunnels and other features were constructed. At one time, railways probably accounted for about a third of brick production in Hampshire; a mile of tunnel required about 14 million bricks.[16] Once completed, the railways enabled bricks to be transported with far greater ease. The industry also became more mechanised, and this led to fewer, larger works, although in Hampshire, in the late 19th century, there were still more than 100 brickworks.[17]

During the present century, many local brickworks have closed; improvements in transport favoured such concerns as the London Brick Company, which now makes almost half the nation's bricks. In Hampshire, bricks are now only made at three places, and on the Isle of Wight the industry has disappeared. Nevertheless, the heritage of brick production in the area, both in terms of brickworks remains and outstanding examples of the product, are considerable.

Probably the most famous bricks to be made in Hampshire were the 'Fareham Reds', used extensively locally in High Street, Fareham, for example, and for the forts on Portsdown Hill, and also in St. Thomas's Hospital, London, the Royal Albert Hall, and the Town Hall in Capetown, South Africa. Nothing is left of the works, which was situated at the south end of Funtley village (SU 565077) – only the product remains.

Little survives either of Blanchards Works, Bishops Waltham (SU 552177), which specialised in terracotta products. The works were in operation for almost a century from the 1860s until 1957. Despite the virtual obliteration of the production area, Blanchards are commemorated by their products which were used for the Prudential offices in Southampton and Portsmouth (SU 420389 and SU 639001), and the brick skin of Hockley Viaduct (see Chapter 7). Further afield, the Grand Hotel, Cairo, Buckingham Palace and the Natural History Museum all feature Blanchards' products.

Some brickworks sites, although disused, retain considerable evidence of their past. At Bailey's Hard, on the Beaulieu estate, for instance, where production ceased in 1934, a good example of a circular down-draught kiln can be seen (SU 394014). The future of Bursledon Brickworks is at present uncertain. The works, which once had a capacity of 20 million bricks a year, its own private railway siding, and four Hoffman kilns, closed some years ago. Dating from 1897, it retains features of considerable interest: in particular a unique drying shed (SU 500101), and it is hoped that part of the complex may be developed as a museum of the brickmaking industry.

On the Isle of Wight, too, it is possible to find reminders of brickmaking. The most interesting is at Northwood, near Cowes, where a small kiln (SZ 471929), formerly part of the Hollis Brick and Tile Works, survives. Production began here in 1856, initially concentrating on field drain pipes, but later expanding into the manufacture of a variety of products before closure in the 1960s. Inside the kiln is a display of some of the wares manufactured by the company. Of the three surviving brickworks in Hampshire, the most unusual is Mr. Pycroft's works on Hayling Island (SU 717035), where small scale production has been going on since 1934, using the clamp method. Mr. Pycroft is a builder, and the bricks he makes are for his own use.

At Selborne, what was a Victorian estate brickworks became a commercial concern in

36. Brick kiln, Baileys Hard.

37. Kiln, Northwood, Isle of Wight.

1934. At this works (SU 767342), bricks are machine made, and the clay is brought from a nearby pit. An interesting cable-worked incline survives, as does part of the Hoffman kilns, now disused; a modern modified Scotch kiln has replaced them.

Perhaps the most interesting of Hampshire's surviving brickworks is that at Michelmersh (SU 343258). Here, bricks are still hand made, and the works specialises in orders for bricks of unusual design. Michelmersh bricks are also well-known for their colour, which encompasses a variety of hues, and examples may be seen at the Nuffield Theatre, Southampton (SU 425154) and in the Courthouse at Romsey (SU 353213). The bricks are fired in circular down-draught oil-fired kilns, 20 feet in diameter, which hold between 35,000 and 38,000 bricks each. They reach a temperature of 1050° C., and it is this heat which helps to produce the distinctive colour of the bricks.

Clay pipe making

This industry was once found in several places in the area, but today not much more than examples of the pipes remain in museums. An important works was at Portchester, near Fareham, which operated from 1813 until 1932. The pipe clay was brought from Devon by barge to nearby Paulsgrove; the chalk for whiting came from Paulsgrove Quarry, the scar of which can be seen above the modern housing estate (SU 635067). The factory building in Portchester survived until c.1970, when the area was redeveloped.[18] In Newport, Isle of Wight, there is one survival of the clay pipe industry: the house of the last clay pipe maker to work on the island.[19]

Chalk-based industries

Various industries associated with the use of chalk operated in the region. Chalk is the raw material for whiting which had many uses: in putty, paint and linoleum, and as an industrial filler and extender and, as mentioned above, for colouring clay pipes. Remains of the industry are scanty, but at some known sites the vast chalk pits serve as a reminder. At Downend, near Fareham (SU 600067), the pit which once supplied the works of Rogers and Cooke (who now produce whiting at a modern plant near Salisbury) remains; a similar relic can be seen beside the A3057 road at Mottisfont, near Romsey (SU 338275).

Lime

Another chalk-based industry of which there are tangible remains is limemaking. Lime was used in building, for water softening, and for agriculture. Chalk was quarried, and quicklime produced by burning it in a kiln. The resulting product could be mixed with water to make slaked lime, used for restoring calcium in soil, or in the manufacture of limewash or mortar. The use of lime for water softening will be dealt with in Chapter 6.

The best surviving traditional limekilns in Hampshire are, without doubt, at Butser, near Petersfield (SU 726205). Built of brick, these have remained in fairly good condition, despite years of disuse. At Old Burghclere (SU 472573), remains of two kilns can be seen, but the site is heavily overgrown and rather dangerous. At Buriton (SU 736198), the chimney and kilns have been demolished, but it is still possible to discover their foundations in the undergrowth.

Cement

The making of cement has never been a Hampshire industry, but an interesting Isle of Wight site is the Medina Cement Works, south of Cowes (SZ 505916). This works was established about 1840 by Charles Francis and Sons. Most of the raw materials were available locally but, even so, some had to be brought in, the goods had to be unloaded on to the specially constructed wharf. The neat little company office building survives, as

38.   Limekiln at Butser, near Petersfield.

39.   Remains of a kiln, Medina Cement Works, Isle of Wight.

do substantial remains of the kilns. Adjacent to the site there are some remains of Cement Mills Halt, on the Cowes to Newport railway line. The bed of the railway is now a footpath. Another cement works on the island was at Brading (SZ 613873), although its active life was short, from c.1850 until the turn of the century. It then fell into disuse, although it re-opened briefly between the wars. A refuse tip now occupies the site.

Glass making

Very little archaeological evidence of this industry can be seen, but at Yarmouth, on the Isle of Wight, a stone building exists (SZ 350897) which was used to store sand from Alum Bay for use in glass manufacture in such centres as Bristol and London. The sand was loaded into vessels through two sets of Gothic-headed doors at the seaward end of the building. It has been established that, in the 16th century, a glasshouse was erected at Buriton, near Petersfield (SU 739168). A survey undertaken in 1971 revealed remains of the works, and in 1972 an excavation confirmed the probable furnace site and other archaeological evidence.[20]

Gunpowder manufacture

A little known site, which is part of Hampshire's industrial heritage, is that of Schultze's Gunpowder Factory at Fritham (SU 228147), in the New Forest. This worked from the mid-1860s until 1923, having the dual advantage of water power and a plentiful supply of charcoal. The rural situation was also an asset, since the buildings were able to be dispersed, reducing the worst consequences of an accident – a common occurrence in such places. The factory specialised in the production of smokeless sporting powder, and at one time employed more than 100 people. The buildings have disappeared, although the remains of some associated housing (see Chapter 9) and the mill pond can be seen.

Chapter Five

Defence Supply and Manufacturing Industries

Although it would be entirely erroneous to claim Hampshire and the Isle of Wight as centres for large scale heavy engineering like the Black Country, nevertheless they are areas with an interesting industrial history in manufacturing and defence supply.

Much of the region's manufacturing has been associated with transport, with shipbuilding, aircraft manufacture and railway engineering all represented. There were, however, a number of individual firms whose reputation for particular products spread far wider than the local area. Armfields of Ringwood, for instance, had an international reputation as millwrights, while Taskers of Andover, and Wallis and Steevens of Basingstoke were also important: Taskers for the manufacture of iron goods of every kind, from bridges to agricultural machinery and traction engines, and Wallis and Steevens for steam vehicles, such as steam rollers and road engines.

The defence supply industry, on the other hand, is somewhat special, and by no means found in every area of the country. For this book, I am including establishments involved in the supply of naval stores, and victualling and armament supply, as well as one very unusual establishment which could be argued to have had a major influence on ship design, although vessels were not actually built there. Portsmouth Dockyard, however, is included both as a centre for shipbuilding and repair, and as a supplier of stores to the Royal Navy.

Manufacturing Industries

In an area with many miles of coastline, shipbuilding has naturally been a feature of both Hampshire and the Isle of Wight for many centuries. There have been several periods, however, when the industry has been especially important. From the late 17th century until the Napoleonic Wars, wooden vessels were built for both naval and merchant service, not only in the dockyard at Portsmouth, but also at Bucklers Hard, Bursledon, various areas of Southampton, and on the Isle of Wight at Cowes and St. Helens. There are but scant remains of this very important phase, since ships of this kind could be built on a beach or river bank, leaving no permanent evidence. The only place where the building of wooden ships offers much in the way of visible evidence is at Bucklers Hard, and even here little has survived of the actual ship construction site. The industrial village has been preserved, though, with rows of brick cottages, some of which have been conserved as illustrations of typical homes of the 1790s (SU 408001). There is also the Master Builder's house, the home of the Adams family, ship builders at Bucklers Hard for many years, and a small chapel. The house is now a restaurant. Not far from the complex is a maritime museum, housed in a modern building (see Appendix 2).

During the 19th century, ship building became an increasingly urban activity, and with technological development the decline of the small yard was inevitable. Apart from the Dockyard, work was concentrated on the River Itchen around Southampton, and at Cowes on the Isle of Wight.

In the 1830s the *Forester*, the first iron ship to be constructed on the Solent, was completed at Millbrook foundry, and launched from the nearby Mill Place Quay. Wooden paddle steamers, such as the *Emerald*, were also being built locally at this time. *Emerald* had the distinction of being the first Southampton-built steam boat and, during her trials in 1830, she achieved the crossing between Hythe and Southampton in 11 minutes.[1]

By 1840, Summers and Co., who had built the *Forester*, had moved their works to Northam, although the Millbrook foundry was retained for building steam engines and railway locomotives for the London and Southampton Railway which had recently opened. During the decade that followed, Summers, Groves and Day (later Day, Summers and Baldock), remained as the only local company engaged in iron shipbuilding, but new yards constructing wooden ships continued to increase in number. Needless to say, the development of Southampton Docks (see Chapter 8) had an impact on the local shipbuilding and repair industry. Vessels were constructed for a number of the great shipping lines, including P & O, and the Royal Mail line.

40. Grasshopper engine at Marvins Boatyard in Cowes, Isle of Wight.

One class of vessel built on the River Itchen will be mentioned more fully in Chapter 8; the steam floating bridges for the Itchen ferry were constructed locally. Yachts were also built and fitted out and still are. In recent years there has been a sad decline in shipbuilding and repair in the Southampton area, although the industry continues in a reduced form. This is also the case on the Isle of Wight, where most of the work undertaken now is on pleasure craft, but there are some interesting survivals. At Cole's Yard at Cowes (SZ 498949), for instance, a patent slip of 1885 may be seen, with its associated equipment, including a grasshopper beam engine housed in an arch under Arctic Road.

One kind of craft associated with the Solent area was a mixture of ship and aircraft: seaplanes and flying boats. Their beginnings date from immediately before the First World War: in 1913 the Cowes firm of J. Samuel White opened an aircraft department. Despite some setbacks this progressed, as did a similar venture undertaken by Saunders Ltd., also of Cowes, working in conjunction with the Sopwith Aviation Company of Kingston-upon-Thames. Their craft, known as 'Bat Boat', was exhibited at the 1913 Olympia Aero Show, and is generally regarded as the first successful flying boat.

Another pioneer was Noel Pemberton-Billing, who established an aircraft factory at Woolston, Southampton, which was known as the Supermarine Works, Pemberton-Billing's idea being that he would produce 'boats that fly, rather than aeroplanes that float'. The manufacture of seaplanes and flying boats was first stimulated by wartime demand, but for several decades remained an important industrial activity in the Solent area.[2] Remains of this are not substantial; much of the Supermarine factory was destroyed by enemy action during the Second World War, and a memorial plaque marks the site (SU 435113). Besides exhibits in Southampton's Hall of Aviation (see Appendix 2), which include a Sandringham Flying Boat, some of the principal survivals are hangars of the Admiralty's First World War flying boat base at Calshot (SU 429077), now used by the U.S. Navy for storage. Imperial House (SU 395123), the terminal for flying boats from 1937 until the war years, can also be seen, as can the later terminal which now serves as HMS Wessex (SU 422106), the Royal Naval Reserve premises. On the Isle of Wight, the gridiron shed, where J.S. White Ltd. constructed their first seaplane in 1913, survives in East Cowes (SZ 501956), a red brick building with corrugated iron roof, and a patent slip adjacent.

41. Gridiron Shed, Cowes, Isle of Wight.

Although the construction and maintenance of aircraft took place in many parts of Britain, the Solent area was in many ways one of the cradles of the industry. Besides the marine aircraft already mentioned, both military and civilian planes were built locally from an early date. What is now the Royal Aircraft Establishment at Farnborough (SU 869545) was formerly the Royal Aircraft Factory, and its earliest beginnings can be traced to the first decade of the century, when the Army's Balloon Factory and School were moved to the site. AVRO opened a factory at Hamble in 1916 (SU 477069); this is now in multiple occupation. A surprising location for aircraft production is the former wool house, currently Southampton Maritime Museum (SU 418111) where in 1910 Eric Moon produced his 'Moonbeam', a single-seater monoplane. Eastleigh Airport (see Chapter 8) was first used in 1918-19, by the U.S. Navy, for aircraft assembly and repair.

Railway engineering, the last of the transport-linked industries in the area, was almost entirely responsible for the growth of Eastleigh. What had been little more than a hamlet mushroomed during the last two decades of the 19th century and the early years of the 20th, following decisions by the London and South Western Railway to move their premises from London. The carriage and wagon works were opened in the late 1880s, and were major employers, with company housing as well as considerable private houses being built (see Chapter 9). The works, to the east of the railway station, closed in 1968 and, although some buildings survive (SU 458192), the site has been much altered for re-use.

42.   The erecting shop at Eastleigh Railway Works.

In 1909 the locomotive works were opened, and for 40 years railway engines were built here.[3] No steam locomotives were built at Eastleigh after 1949, but heavy repairs continued until 1966, with a light Pacific locomotive, No. 34089, being the last steam locomotive to pass through the erecting shop.[4] The works are still in use, however, for the repair and maintenance of diesel and electric rolling stock (SU 458185).

No locomotives were ever built on the Isle of Wight but, not surprisingly, facilities for the maintenance and repair of stock were provided; an early repair shop at Cowes and, in 1891, workshops at Newport.[5] Since 1923, the whole island system has been served by workshops adjacent to the station at St. John's Road, Ryde (SZ 596919).

Manufacturing industry in Hampshire was not confined to transport. What later became Armfield's of Ringwood was established in c.1840, under the control of one William Munden, who did agricultural engineering and millwrighting.[6] Joseph Armfield went into partnership with Munden in 1876 and before long took sole control, although the name Munden, Armfield and Co. continued to be used for some years. In 1882, the company took over the Stuckton Iron Works, which provided them with a much larger foundry than they then possessed in Ringwood. Later, this works was devoted to agricultural engineering only. Around the turn of the century, Armfield's established a national and later international reputation as manufacturers of mill machinery and, in particular, water turbines. Armfield's also gave Ringwood a place in the early history of wireless telegraphy,[7] by building apparatus for Marconi at their Vale of Avon Ironworks.

Armfield's products were various, including lamp posts and inspection covers, as well as their more famous mill items. After Joseph Armfield's death in 1935, his son took over the business, but by the 1940s shortage of labour and materials had caused the company difficulties, and the major part of the works was sold to Wellworthy Ltd. In 1953, the Stuckton works was also sold. Most of the buildings on this site survive (SU 160134), but Armfield's main works have been demolished. However, the buildings of Munden's smithy (SU 152047), where Armfield first began trading, still stand and, nearby, the cottages in Duck Island Lane were used at one time by William Munden for making farm and mill machinery.

Another well-known Hampshire engineering company was Taskers of Andover. The Tasker brothers built the Waterloo Ironworks in the early 19th century, at first producing agricultural implements such as ploughs, but it is for their traction engines that the company are justly famous. In 1968, Taskers were taken over and now the Anna Valley Works is empty. Little survives of the complex, except for the Workmen's Hall of 1867 (SU 343440), and some workers' housing (see Chapter 9).

The firm of Wallis and Steevens originated in the 1840s with the Wallis brothers who were ironmongers, ironfounders and agricultural manufacturers in Basingstoke.[8] In 1856 the new North Hants Ironworks was opened, and it was about a decade later that Charles Steevens joined the company. At this time they were agents for several machine makers, besides manufacturing farm machinery themselves. Later they became internationally famous as makers of steam engines, rollers and tractors, producing more than 6,000 engines between the 1870s and 1940.[9] In recent years they adapted their trade to changing times and made diesel units, but in 1981 the company ceased trading and the works closed. Nothing of industrial archaeological significance remains – the company had moved to new premises in 1967 and the old works were demolished soon afterwards. Nevertheless, their products survive as reminders of a chapter in Hampshire's industrial history.

Defence Supply

Since the end of the 15th century, the fortunes of Portsmouth and its dockyard have been closely intertwined.[10] Although the waters of Portsmouth harbour had long been used to lay up ships, the beginnings of a permanent navy date only from the Tudor period. It was in the 1490s that King Henry VII ordered that a dry dock be constructed at Portsmouth; it was the first such structure in the country and was situated near where HMS *Victory* lies today.[11]

Gradually, as a collection of storehouses and workshops were erected, the dockyard evolved. It was not, however, until the end of the 17th century that it became important, as the wars with France and Spain resulted in its gaining preference over yards nearer to London. In the 1690s work began, under the direction of Edward Dummer, Surveyor of the Navy Board. A new dry dock (Henry VII's dock had long since been filled in) was built, known as the Great Stone Dock (SU 628007). Its design was revolutionary, having stone-stepped sides, previous dry docks being of wood with vertical walls. These had leaked, and proved unstable, and access to them was inconvenient.[12] In 1769, this dock was rebuilt, slightly to the east, but apart from alterations to its entrance and head, it was little changed from Dummer's design, and survives today.[13] Investment in Portsmouth Dockyard continued in the early years of the 18th century, and survivals of this period include a fine collection of houses (SU 633007), built between 1715 and 1719 for officers of the Dockyard.[14] By the 1720s, when Daniel Defoe recorded his impressions of Portsmouth, its vital role in defence was well known, it having 'the best security to the Navy above all the places in Britain'.[15] Defoe noted that the 'docks and yards are now like a town by themselves',[16] and the economic significance of this did not escape his attention. He commented that Portsmouth, 'besides its being a fortification, is a well inhabited, thriving, prosperous corporation; and hath been greatly enrich'd of late by the fleet's having so often and so long lay there . . . besides the constant fitting out of men here . . . these things have not only been a great advantage to the town, but has [sic] really made the whole place rich'.[17]

43.   Storehouses at Portsmouth Naval Base.

By this time, Portsmouth Dockyard was the largest in the country in terms of manpower, with more than 1,000 employed there.[18] There was a short lull in building, with little money for investment available, but the second half of the 18th century witnessed considerable developments, and a number of the yard's finest buildings date from this period. A serious fire in 1770 led to a reassessment of the form these buildings should take; consequently structures were mainly of brick rather than wood, as previously. One fine range of buildings dating from this time are the storehouses, formerly Nos. 9, 10 and 11 Stores, which line the route taken by visitors to HMS *Victory* and the *Mary Rose*. These were of simple but sturdy internal design and have three floors, an attic and a cellar. Built of red brick, with a central pediment edged in Portland stone, this series of storehouses provides an impressive vista along the main road from Victory Gate.[19] Other buildings from the period include a line of three hemp stores (SU 630005), the Hatchelling House of 1771 (SU 633006) where hemp was prepared for ropemaking, and the Great Ropery itself (SU 628005-632005). This structure, 1,095 feet long, was completed in 1776, spinning taking place on the upper floors,

44. Block Mills, Portsmouth Naval Base.

45. No. 2 Ship Shop, Portsmouth Naval Base.

with the ground floor being used for rope winding. It survives today as No.18 store, ropemaking having ceased at Portsmouth in 1868.[20]

What might be termed 'workers' housing' had not been neglected in the latter part of the 18th century. Admiralty House (SU 633004) is a fine mansion designed by Samuel Wyatt, built in the 1780s at a cost of more than £15,000. On a rather more modest scale but of similar date is Short Row (SU 633006), a terrace for such senior yard officials as the Surgeon and the Master Ropemaker.[21]

The early years of the 19th century also marked a phase of development in Portsmouth Dockyard, in particular for the construction of a series of dry docks.[22] The building known as the Block Mills (SU 628008) is of a rather functional design, but holds an important place in industrial history. Here were housed the machines, designed by Marc Brunel (father of Isambard Kingdom Brunel), which constitute the world's first example of metal machine tools for mass production.[23]

Following the end of the wars with France in 1815, little building was undertaken in the Portsmouth yard for some years. It is possible to trace dockyard development in relation to the international situation: in times of tension or war, building work accelerated; with the coming of peace, the pace of activity slowed down. The next phase of expansion, however, occurred because of changing technology, rather than the demands of hostilities. By the 1840s, steam propulsion for naval vessels was gaining in importance, and facilities to build and repair such ships were needed. Further land reclamation took place, and what was known as the 'Great Steam Basin' (No. 2 Basin) was opened by Queen Victoria in 1848. This survives, flanked by one of the Dockyard's most attractive buildings, the Steam Factory, now known as No. 2 Ship Shop (SU 629010). Six hundred feet long, it is of red brick, with Portland stone decoration, and fine metal framed windows.[24]

Other dockyard buildings of the time include the Fire Station (SU 630006), of corrugated iron on a cast iron framework, the Chain Testing Shop (SU 627003) and No. 6 Boathouse (SU 630004) a fine stone structure with a notable internal construction.[25]

A further extension to the yard took place in the latter part of the 19th century and the years leading up to the First World War, when about 95 acres of land were reclaimed[26] and vast works undertaken. This area, still in defence use, and to which public access is extremely limited, is even today known as the Extension Area. The buildings there include a Factory (SU 639009), constructed in 1905 in connection with the Dreadnought building programme; a red brick structure covering a vast floor area.[27]

In recent years, changes in defence requirements have resulted in the contraction of the naval role of Portsmouth Dockyard – now officially a Fleet Maintenance Base. Most of its historic buildings however, have been preserved, and public access made easier, especially in what is now the Heritage Area close to Victory Gate. Attempts are being made to develop the tourist potential of the Dockyard, and this was assisted in 1987 by the arrival of HMS *Warrior*, the first ironclad, now displayed adjacent to Victory Gate and open to visitors.

Although the role of Portsmouth Dockyard has had little effect on the industrial history of the Isle of Wight, the same cannot be said for other parts of Hampshire. The most important of these is undoubtedly Gosport, where fine historic industrial buildings may be seen. At R.N.A.D. Priddys Hard, for example, the building which now houses the Museum of Ordnance was erected for a quite different purpose. Originally, gunpowder storage had been in Old Portsmouth, in the Square Tower, but fears of explosion coupled with a need for additional space resulted in its removal to Gosport where a magazine was built remote from dwellings. This building, called the Great Magazine (SU 616012), was erected in the 1770s, and was designed in a manner appropriate to its function.[28] Access to the museum is currently restricted, although visits are possible by appointment (see Appendix 2).

Also in Gosport is the Royal Clarence Victualling Yard, which includes a number of

46. Fire Station, Portsmouth Naval Base.

47. No. 6 Boathouse at Portsmouth Naval Base.

48. Mill and granary complex, Royal Clarence Yard.

49. Slaughterhouse, Royal Clarence Yard.

fine industrial buildings, all now re-used for other purposes. Amongst the earliest buildings to survive is the single-storey cooperage (SU 617005) which remained in use until the abolition of the naval rum issue in 1970. Before closure a film was made recording its activities. Although a number of buildings were destroyed by enemy action in the Second World War, there are some noteworthy 19th-century survivals. The most impressive is unquestionably the red brick complex of bakery, mill and granary (SU 618007) which stands on the edge of the wharf. Designed by the Navy Board Architect, G.L. Taylor, these buildings date from 1828-32. Despite their survival, there is but scant remains of the machinery which was once to be found inside.[29] Nearby is the former slaughterhouse (SU 618008) which dates from the 1850s and is similar in design to contemporary buildings in the dockyard. Other features, which reveal the structure's original use, are still visible, and brick cattle sheds also survive to the west.[30]

A little known piece of defence supply heritage may be seen at what is now the Admiralty Marine Technology Establishment. This is one of the world's earliest ship model tanks (SU 613986), dating from 1886 and designed by R.E. Froude. Memorabilia of Froude, and of his father William, are located in a museum on the site, and this may been visited by appointment.

Without doubt, the largest industrial building in Hampshire is the structure at Woolston, Southampton, known as the 'Rolling Mills' (SU 439101). It was built during the First World War, and its early history is shrouded, to some degree, in mystery, although it is certain that some munitions manufacture took place there. Between the wars, the site was used for various purposes, but for more than 40 years, since the Second World War, it was a Naval Store Depot, housing bulky items like cable, as an outstation of Portsmouth Dockyard. It is now disused and its future, at the time of writing, is uncertain. Almost half a mile long, it is a very impressive structure, but one for which finding a new use would be difficult. The issue has been complicated by the discovery of toxic waste on the site.

Chapter Six

Public Utilities

It is very easy to take what may be termed 'Public Utilities' – the supply of gas, electricity and water, and the disposal of waste water – for granted. The historic remains of these services are often not considered as part of our industrial heritage; they are nonetheless very important, having an effect not only on the quality of life, but also on public health.

Within the last 150 years, the development of public utilities has progressed apace. Although a few places, including Southampton, had a primitive water supply, it was not until the 19th century that the link was made between pure water and the effective disposal of waste and the health of the community. The use of gas, first for lighting and later for cooking and heating, dates from the last century, too, and many places had no electricity supply until well into the 20th century. Nevertheless, change has been so rapid that the early buildings and artefacts associated with public utilities have generally become redundant and, if we are to preserve examples as part of our industrial heritage, a policy for doing so will have to be pursued actively before too much is lost.

Gas

As with so many industries, it is difficult to be definite about the date of the first use of gas, initially for illumination. It was certainly known by the latter part of the 17th century that gas could be extracted from coal and other fuels and put to advantageous use. It was, however, another hundred years before serious experiments were made. Hugh Barty-King mentions the work of Archibald Cochrane, Earl of Dundonald, who inherited an estate at Culross in Scotland in 1778. In an attempt to revive his family fortunes, he tried to exploit the local natural resource, coal. While turning this into coke, he produced coal gas and, to dispose of this safely, he diverted it from the top of his kilns through discarded gun barrels, setting it alight to be sure of avoiding any chance of explosion. The flame could be seen across the Firth of Forth, and Dundonald produced a curiosity which he placed in his hall: a vessel burning coal gas and producing illumination. He did not, unfortunately, realise the potential of his creation, and it remained simply an amusement for visitors.[1]

The first person to recognise the possibilities of combustion by mixing coal gas and air was William Murdock, principal engine erector in Cornwall for Boulton and Watt. He undertook a number of experiments in the 1790s (one of which resulted in the lighting of a room in his house in Redruth by gas), but it was not until the beginning of the 19th century that he began to consider the commercial potential of his work.[2] Before long, Boulton and Watt were producing a gas-making plant using Murdock's horizontal retort, and in 1812 the first general gas company, the London Gas, Light and Coke Company, was established.

By 1850, many towns had their own gasworks, with mains distributing the gas to both domestic and industrial customers. For some years gas was used almost entirely for lighting, but this was a major development, since it enabled towns to install reliable street lighting for the first time. In the second half of the 19th century gas came to be used for other purposes, with gas cookers available from c.1850, hot water geysers from 1865, gas rings from 1867, and gas fires from 1880.

Until the tapping of natural gas revolutionised the industry, the process usually used coal as its main raw material, although experiments were done to produce gas from oil. Traditional gas production plants may still be seen, preserved in museum form, at Biggar in Scotland and Fakenham in Norfolk, but unfortunately nowhere in the area covered by this book. There are, though, a number of features of the industry's heritage in Hampshire and the Isle of Wight.

Southampton first had gas lighting in 1820, the contract being let to the company of Barlow Brothers. In the early years the innovation was very controversial as many people feared that gasholders might explode, and sites for works were chosen, whenever possible, to avoid densely populated areas. Southampton has two of the finest surviving gasholders in the county, at Northam (SU 429122). One is a column guided holder from 1902, with a capacity of two million cubic feet, in two lifts; the other is a four-lift spiral guided holder from 1935, which can hold three and a half million cubic feet. Nearby is a block of apartments built for the employees at the works (see Chapter 9).

Both in Southampton and Lymington, columns commemorating lighting with gas survive, although neither is on its original site. That in Southampton (SU 425116), stands near Hoglands Park, and is an ornate structure in cast iron, bearing an inscription recording the gift to the town by William Chamberlayne, a local Member of Parliament, of the original gas street lamp posts. The column at Lymington once stood in the centre of the town, but has now been moved to the car park of the Yacht Club (SZ 332952).

Gasholders, now largely redundant, are a feature gradually disappearing from towns and cities. In Hampshire a number survive, for instance at Fareham (SU 585060), where two small spiral guided examples may be seen. This is the second gasworks site in Fareham; the first, which opened in 1836 to the north of the town, proved to be somewhat unsatisfactory. Local gas was very expensive, but this was overcome by the choice of the new site by the quay where coal could be unloaded for the works, straight from ships. A large column guided gasholder can be seen at Aldershot (SU 882501), dating from the mid-1920s. It is unusually tall, with five lifts. Another holder survives at Gosport, rather smaller in size (SZ 612993), as does one as Emsworth (SU 749061). The Isle of Wight recently lost a fine gasholder at St. Helens (SZ 628886), although another at Newport (SZ 502894) does survive.

A century ago, the gasholder was a common site, but the increased use of electricity, coupled with nationalisation in 1949, led to a streamlining of the industry; the introduction of natural gas changed distribution arrangements dramatically. A few remains of the traditional gas industry, besides those already mentioned, can be seen in Hampshire and on the Isle of Wight. On the island, for instance, the former offices of Ryde Gasworks, now in residential use, survive in Park Road (SZ 597922), with the former purifier house nearby occupied, somewhat ironically, by the Southern Electricity Board. At Havenstreet (SZ 555898), a retort house of 1886 is still to be seen, although its gasholder has long since disappeared. The gasworks here were a private venture, financed by a local benefactor to serve the village.

On the mainland, similar scattered items of gas industry heritage can be seen. Although most of Portsmouth's gasworks have disappeared, the foundation stone survives, just to the west of the entrance to the present Hilsea works. This bears the date 1905 and lists the board at that time of the Portsea Island Gas Light Company (SU 664029). At Havant, two original buildings of 1856 (SU 721066) are now used by a building firm.[3] At Hartley Wintney the retort house of 1861 has been altered, but still stands on the west side of Hare's Lane (SU 769575).

Probably the most attractive reminders of the era of gaslighting are the surviving lamp posts. Although usually converted for use with electricity, many of these standards are highly decorative, and retain their distinctive ladder arms. A delightful collection may be seen at New Alresford (SU 588329), although these originally came from Reading. A rare example is near to the cathedral in Winchester (SU 480293). This is kept alight night and

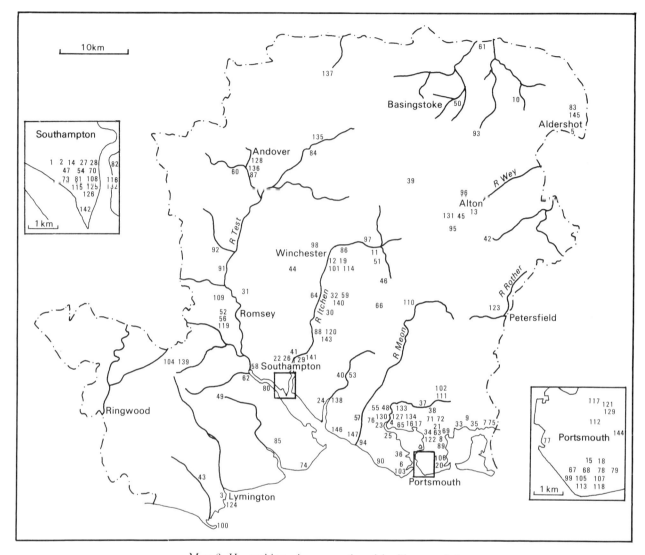

Map 9. Hampshire places mentioned in Chapters 6-9.

KEY

1. Gasholders, Northam, Southampton
2. Gas column, Southampton
3. Gas column, Lymington
4. Gasholder, Fareham
5. Gasholder, Aldershot
6. Gasholder, Gosport
7. Gasholders, Emsworth
8. Portsmouth gasworks site

9. Havant gasworks
10. Retort House, Hartley Wintney
11. Lamp, New Alresford
12. Lamp, Winchester
13. Lamp, Alton
14. Power station sites, Southampton
15. Power station site, Portsmouth

16. Power station, Fareham
17. Lamp, Fareham
18. Lamps, Southsea
19. Garnier Road Pumping Station, Winchester
20. Eastney Pumping Station
21. Cosham booster pumping station
22. Stench pipe, Southampton

50. Gasholder at Newport, Isle of Wight.

51. Former gasworks, Ryde, Isle of Wight.

52. Retort House, Havenstreet, Isle of Wight.

day, being a Webb's Patent Sewage Gas Destructor, dating from the 1880s: besides providing illumination, it also serves to ventilate a sewer. A similar lamp can be seen in Alton (SU 707389).

On the Isle of Wight, a working gas lamp survives at Northwood (SZ 470934); other visible examples have been converted to electric power. At Shide Cross, Newport (SZ 499883), a very ornate fluted column stands with both its ladder arms virtually intact, its base decorated with four shields bearing lions rampant. A most unusual lamp standard is that which, combined with a water trough, is at the junction of West Street and Swanmore Road, Ryde. Dating from 1888, it was given by a local benefactress.

Electricity

Since it is only just over a century since Faraday first demonstrated the possibility of generating electric power, the study of the heritage of electricity generation is frequently overlooked. The first major generating stations were erected in the 1880s and 1890s, hand powered equipment being used for the previous few decades. As Lord Briggs has pointed out, electricity as a power source (as opposed to use for communications), was not adopted so readily in England as it was in countries like Germany and the United States of America.[4] Britain tended to 'cling to steam', and it is perhaps not surprising that most early electricity undertakings were, like gas, owned by private companies. In the last years of the 19th century, however, municipal involvement became increasingly common. As is the

53. Gas lamp, Northwood, Isle of Wight.

case in so many industries, increases in scale have transformed electricity supply, and the creation in the 1930s of the National Grid, together with post-war nationalisation, has resulted in far fewer stations, transmitting over long distances. Nationally, the tendency is for coal fired stations to be within reach of their fuel. For nuclear power stations, location is normally determined by the need for cooling water, and a preference for sites as remote as possible from habitation.

In Hampshire today, Fawley Power Station is the only place generating electricity for public supply. In bygone days, however, more than twenty stations worked in the county, as well as a number on the Isle of Wight, and some remains are still visible.

The Southampton Electric Light and Power Company first provided lighting in 1888, continuing to do so until a Corporation take-over in 1896. By the turn of the century, electric street lighting had been introduced, and the street tramways began to be similarly powered. Both the power stations of 1896/7 (SU 422113) and that of 1903 (SU 415121) have been demolished, and there is little left to remind us of the early days of electricity supply in Southampton.

Similarly, Portsmouth Power Station, opened in 1894, was demolished in recent years (SZ 631996). Other sites have fared better. At Fareham, for instance, the town's generating station on the Lower Quay survives (SU 578058). The building's position was influenced by the ease of bringing coal supplies by water (as with the gasworks) and it functioned from 1897 until 1932. It is now used for industry. Also in Fareham is a fine set of early electric street lamp standards of ornate design. Standing in the High Street (SU 583065), several of these were installed to commemorate Queen Victoria's Diamond Jubilee in 1897, with others being added soon after. Similarly a set of ornate Edwardian lighting columns grace the seafront at Southsea (SZ 653981-674989). These standards, bearing the former town crest of Portsmouth, are of slightly differing designs, but all have at their head two lanterns suspended on brackets.

On the Isle of Wight, as on the mainland, most of the evidence of electricity supply history has been lost. Within the last few years, the former Skew Bridge Works at Lake (SZ 588828),[5] which dated from 1902, and was later used as an ice-cream factory, has been demolished. The generating station at Ventnor, however, has survived, and can be seen not far from the former railway station site (SZ 563777). There is a most interesting and unusual street lamp at Seaview (SZ 610918), with a large rectangular base, surmounted by a short column and marked 'Seaview Electricity Supply'.

Sewage Disposal

Although hardly a romantic subject, the disposal of waste matter is quite literally a matter of life and death. Until the mid-18th century, it posed no serious problem, although urban conditions were often extremely unpleasant. As increased industrial production and population growth resulted in a great deal more waste, it became clear, however, that initiatives would be needed to deal with its disposal.

In theory, London had a system of waste disposal from the mid-17th century onwards but, in practice, conditions were not much improved and, furthermore, in the provinces virtually no developments occurred at this time. The first half of the 19th century witnessed some change in attitude, especially as the link between adequate waste disposal and public health came to be known. A series of cholera epidemics resulted in a general feeling that something must be done; progress was, nevertheless, very slow. The first real action to be taken was the passing, in 1845, of the Sewage and Drainage of Towns Act, but many authorities were very tardy in implementing this legislation. Conditions in urban areas were at this time quite appalling. A report compiled in 1848 about Portsmouth describes a typical scene in a working class area with only open ditches in which waste could be disposed of: 'the accumulation of filth in that ditch has been going on for nineteen years. It has been emptied once in this time . . . It smells most intolerable in hot weather. There have been cases of fever in this district'.[6] In 1851 in Portsmouth, 25 of every 1,000 people died each year, an unacceptably high mortality rate, but scarcely surprising in the circumstances.

During the 1860s and 1870s many sewage pumping stations were erected. These did not treat the waste in any way; the first sewage treatment did not occur until the 1880s. Even so, the removal of waste in sewers assisted considerably in improving the state of towns. Rivers were less polluted and the horrific stench in the streets reduced. Pumping stations were needed because of the inadequacy of most gradients to carry the waste away by gravity.

The most remarkable aspect of Victorian pumping stations was their architecture. Whereas today a functional structure would be provided, in the 19th century it was regarded as proper that such buildings should be as decorative as they were useful. Many are reminiscent of cathedrals, aesthetically attractive and enormous in scale. Even the machinery was very special: beam engines were both splendid with decorative ironwork and graceful in motion.

54. Former Ventnor Electricity Works.

55. Skew Bridge Electricity Works, Lake, Isle of Wight.

In Hampshire there are substantial remains of buildings and machinery associated with the history of sewage disposal. Although Winchester was a late starter in this field, its pumping station of 1878 survives in Garnier Road (SU 480282). The building required extensions as the population increased, and these date from 1904, 1910, and 1930, as recorded on several datestones. The original steam engines, built by Gimson of Leicester, have long since been removed. Interestingly, from 1910 steam was raised in the Babcock and Wilcox boilers by burning refuse, a practice which continued until 1975.

56.   Eastney Pumping Station, Portsmouth.

The history of Portsmouth's drainage system is of some interest in that there is very little gradient. The first pumping station was opened at Eastney (SZ 673992) in 1868. Here a pair of Clayton beam engines raised the waste into an outfall pipe.[7] The building survives and is now used as a workshop; its machinery has been removed. In the early 1880s it was realised that a larger system was needed to cope with the increase in population. In May 1887, a fine engine house was opened, containing a pair of 150 h.p. two cylinder compound beam engines, made by James Watt and Co. The building, which bears a datestone, is ecclesiastical in design with attractive round-headed windows, complete with iron glazing bars. The engines remain intact, although now only used for demonstration purposes. The complex is administered by Portsmouth City Museums and is open to the public, frequently with one engine in steam (see Appendix 2). The opening of this building, a century ago, was as ostentatious as its architecture. A delightful account in a contemporary newspaper,[8] tells in picturesque language of the dignitaries descending the tanks, lit by thousands of

Vauxhall lamps, and gathering to witness 'the actual contact of the sewage with the sea'. After the ceremonies, the very large party of local worthies moved in procession to the 'bijou theatre' of the local lunatic asylum, which had been lavishly decorated for the occasion. Here they enjoyed lunch, and listened to speeches on the customary themes equating cleanliness with godliness and other virtues.

Despite the scale on which the 1887 engine house at Eastney had been built, it proved necessary to add to its pumping capacity within 20 years. In 1904, three horizontally opposed Crossley gas engines were installed. As Dr. Riley observes, the buildings which house these are relatively nondescript,[9] a reflection of the beginning of modern attitudes to public utilities. Two electric engine houses began operating in 1922 and 1939; pumping is now done in modern premises nearby. A number of booster stations erected between 1909 and the 1930s also survive, as that at Cosham (SU 664049), which unlike most 20th-century installations is of architectural merit.[10]

57. Stench pipe at Bursledon.   58. Drainhole cover, Shanklin, Isle of Wight.

There are other reminders of the development of waste disposal in the county. Some often go unnoticed: stench pipes, erected to enable concentrations of sewer gas to escape safely, can be seen at many places. A cast iron example stands on the corner of Glen Eyre Road, Southampton (SU 423156); it was supplied by Adams of York. Another iron pipe stands in Highlands Road, Fareham (SU 576046), and at Bursledon (SU 486094), not far from the railway station, a concrete stench pipe survives. Perhaps the most remarkable pipe is that in Gosport Road, Fareham (SU 576055), near to the *Bird in Hand* public house. This doubled as a stench pipe and a traction pole to support the overhead wires for the trams which ran between Gosport and Fareham (see Chapter 7). Drainhole covers, too, can prove interesting. Many of these were produced in local foundries: that in Bassett Crescent East, Southampton (SU 420157) was made by Harland and Wolff during a slack period in their trading. Other interesting covers survive at a variety of locations across the county.

On the Isle of Wight, the history of waste disposal has left relics similar to those on the mainland. At Newport, near to the quayside (SZ 501894), a small brick pumping station survives, bearing a datestone of 1895. Motive power was probably by gas or diesel engines. Stench pipes, too, may be seen on the island, and at Shanklin there are a number of drainhole covers made in a Newport foundry (for example at SZ 585814).

Although today we may be a little amused at the Victorian attitude to drainage, the results of its development should never be underestimated. A century after the time when Portsmouth's death rate was 25 per 1,000, it had fallen to about 11 per 1,000. Many features contributed to this of course, but nevertheless, proper waste disposal was a vital element in the improvement.[11]

Water Supply

A reliable and pure water supply is essential to our quality of life. It is difficult to imagine that, even in urban areas, such a supply has only been available in relatively recent times, yet this is so. Before the industrial revolution, water supply posed few problems in a county like Hampshire, or on the Isle of Wight, with many fast-flowing rivers and streams, supplemented by local wells as necessary, providing sufficient quantities for everyone. In rural areas, water was often raised by the use of man, animal or windpower.

The 19th-century increase in industrial activity and in population necessitated a more sophisticated system, and it is from this time that most piped systems in the area date. These, like waste disposal arrangements, have usually been provided by municipal bodies, although a few private companies have been, and indeed remain, active.

Hampshire was unusual in having piped water in one place, Southampton, from a much earlier date. From the Middle Ages, water from springs was carried to a waterhouse, and from there conveyed by lead pipes to the Friary, near God's House Tower.[12] Of this arrangement, which was in municipal ownership from 1420, the waterhouse survives (SU 415124), a stone building opposite the Mayflower Theatre.

In the early 19th century increased demand led to the investigation of alternative sources of water for Southampton. From the 1830s, attempts were made to obtain water froom beneath Southampton Common and, in addition, reservoirs were constructed on the Common to collect surface water. Although all these proved inadequate, they have left an interesting legacy. Of the original reservoirs (as distinct from the modern ones still in use), remains of No. 3 and No. 2 can be seen. The No. 3 reservoir (built c.1832) now forms a boating lake (SU 417144), while No. 2 (built c.1811) is part of a children's paddling pool (SU 418141). Of the Deep Well, where boring began in 1838 and did not finally cease until 1883, an inscribed stone slab marks its site (SU 417145). Water was found here, but the yield was less than anticipated, although the borehole had reached a depth of 1,317 feet before being abandoned.

By the middle of the 19th century, it was realised that a water pumping station to serve Southampton was essential, and this was established at Mansbridge, the water being extracted from the river Itchen, with Cornish engines pumping it to the reservoirs on the Common. The pumping station, however, was not in use for long, as the supply was polluted by effluent from upstream, and in 1888 it was abandoned in favour of the wells at Otterbourne. Of the building itself, nothing but a few stones, which may have been part of the foundations, survives (SU 448158). Remains of the adjacent reservoir may be seen, as well as some company housing (see Chapter 9).

The Otterbourne Pumping Station came into use at the end of the 1880s, and contained during its life a variety of steam plant, including a compound beam engine of 1896, and a pair of Worthington Simpson triple expansion engines dating from 1926. All of this, together with the historic buildings, has now disappeared, and a modern works operates on the site (SU 468233).

The South Hants. Water Company opened its first pumping station at Timsbury in 1876. Its original buildings housed two small beam engines, with an addition dated 1897 providing accommodation for a larger steam engine, which was later replaced by diesel and electric machinery. With modern water pumping being done by electric submersible pumps, Timsbury Works, which had been operated since 1921 by Southampton Corporation Water-works and from 1974 by the Southern Water Authority, no longer required its original buildings (SU 346255), and these were demolished in 1982.

A rare survival of a small rural water pumping station is that at Twyford (SU 493248). Like the Timsbury Works, it was constructed by the South Hants. Water Company, and then administered in turn by Southampton Corporation and the Southern Water Authority. Its earliest buildings date from 1900, with additions bearing datestones of 1905, 1912 and 1934. The site, which includes five bottle-shaped limekilns and associated plant, is a scheduled Ancient Monument, and the buildings have been considerably renovated in recent years. Currently the machinery, including a Hathorn Davey triple expansion steam engine and diesel engines, is being restored by volunteers, and the pumping station holds regular Open Days, besides receiving visitors by appointment (see Appendix 2).

The use of lime was necessary before modern detergents were available, since it was very difficult to work up a lather with soap in areas of hard water. At Twyford, chalk was quarried from a pit behind the main building and carried in small trucks up to the kilns on a rope-worked incline. Coal was similarly transported, and lime was produced by burning the chalk, with the coal used as fuel. Lime was then slaked to make 'cream of lime', and used to soften the water, the deposit being removed by filtration. Unfortunately the filtration equipment at Twyford has been removed, although the building survives.

Other areas of Hampshire also have an interesting water supply history. In Portsmouth, for example, from 1811 until 1840, two rival companies competed: the Portsea Island Company and the Farlington Company.[13] On 25 March 1840 they combined to form the United Portsmouth, Portsea and Farlington Waterworks Company, later being bought out by the Borough of Portsmouth Waterworks Company. These various changes led to considerable improvements in supply to the inhabitants of Portsmouth. When the two rival companies were operational, supply was only provided for a few hours daily, and there were serious misgivings expressed concerning the purity of the water.

A number of sites in the Portsmouth area reveal remains of the history of local water supply. The earliest of these is the brick walled Drayton Basin of 1812 (SU 678058).[14] Pumping stations survive, including those at Drayton (SU 678058), dating from 1905, and Portsbridge (SU 655047) from 1929. Also in the south east of the county is one of the most attractive relics: the massive terracotta brick pump house at Havant (SU 710063). Although this now contains electric motors, which replaced the original Worthington Simpson triple expansion engines of the 1920s, it is an architectural gem, designed by the local architect, A.E. Cogswell.[15] Of the original works on the site, dating from 1860, only the gatehouse remains.

Another works dating from 1860 was that at Bury Cross, Gosport (SU 598996). This ceased pumping in 1907, when activity was transferred to Soberton, near Wickham. At Gosport, some buildings survive; at Soberton (SU 596143), only the chimney has been demolished. The engines here were of horizontal rather than vertical design, which is reflected in the low profile of the engine house.

59. Twyford Pumping Station.

60. Limekilns at Twyford Pumping Station.

More water pumping stations survive in Hampshire,[16] but other items associated with water supply include handpumps, such as those at Southwick (SU 627087), and at Preston Candover (SU 607416) where it stands conspicuously on a brick platform on the village green. Drinking fountains are not uncommon, nor are horse troughs, though most are now disused. Many drinking fountains were erected to commemorate the Diamond Jubilee of Queen Victoria in 1897 as at Botley (SU 521132) and in Southampton (SU 443151). One fountain of slightly earlier date, and very unusual design, is that at Selborne (SU 744329). The iron fountain, cast by MacFarlane and Co., a Scottish foundry, dates from 1879, and is in the shape of a lion's head, the mouth discharging water into a trough. Next to it is a round-headed door, behind which is an hydraulic ram which pumped water into a reservoir serving standpipes in the village, there being no piped water supply until 1934. This system, financed by public subscription in 1894 in memory of the local naturalist, Gilbert White, continued to serve some remote dwellings until the 1960s.

On the Isle of Wight a most interesting example of an old waterworks building can be seen at Ventnor (SZ 562777). Dating from the 1880s, it is a typical Victorian public utility structure, but a particular feature is the decorative nature of its bargeboards. Until recently another fascinating example could be seen at Knighton, where derelict beam engine houses and a former gas engine house remained; demolition has recently taken place and much of the site's historic interest has been lost. Also on the island are a number of handpumps such as those at Yarmouth (SZ 354896), and at Brading (SZ 606871) which dates from 1764. An attractive and unusual survival is the set of ornate water standards in the village of Whitwell (SZ 521778 and 523781 among others). These were installed by a local benefactor in 1887 and are now painted a distinctive red.

Few water towers were necessary in Hampshire and on the Isle of Wight, since the undulating terrain generally allowed reservoirs to be built at sufficient height. Of those that were built, one good example is at New Milton (SZ 244952). Although even most remote rural areas now have piped water, this is a comparatively recent development, and wind, human and animal power were used to raise water from wells. The windpump, once common, has become a rare sight (see Chapter 2).

Animal engines in Hampshire and on the Isle of Wight can be fitted into two main classifications: those in which an animal moves in a circle around a point in a horizontal plane, and those in which motion, of man or beast, is in a vertical plane.[17] An interesting example of the former can be seen at Lainston House, Sparsholt (SU 441316) where, in an outhouse, there is a horse wheel which raised water from a well 360 feet deep. At Donkey

61. Handpump, Preston Candover.   62. Former drinking fountain in Botley.

63. Former Waterworks, Ventnor, Isle of Wight.   64. Water standard, Whitwell, Isle of Wight.

65. Horse wheel, Lainston House, near Winchester.

Well Lane, Beech (SU 687386), encased in a timber building on a brick base, a vertical wheel, 12 feet in diameter, survives. Although the place name confirms that animal power was used here, as Kenneth Major points out, being a communal wheel, it could equally have been worked using human power.[18] A treadwheel which was definitely man-operated is that at Beauworth (SU 570246), in what is now *The Milburys* public house and restaurant. This also has a diameter of 12 feet and is 3 ft. 8 ins. wide; its position is such that the use of animal power would not have been practicable. There is only one bucket on the windlass, suggesting that it may have been operated by one man alone.[19] On the Isle of Wight, there is probably one of the best known animal-powered machines for lifting water, at Carisbrooke Castle, where a donkey wheel still operates for the benefit of tourists (SZ 487876). The well dates from 1150; the wheel and its wheel house were rebuilt in 1587.[20]

Chapter Seven

Transport I: Road and Rail

Transport history is a very important part of our industrial heritage, and touches virtually every other industry. Hampshire and the Isle of Wight are somewhat different from each other in terms of their development: Hampshire transport was concerned both with travel around the county and also for through traffic, such as that which involved Southampton docks. Transport on the Isle of Wight was more self contained. The whole area, however, has a varied and rich transport heritage and for this reason it will be dealt with in two chapters: this one devoted to land transport and Chapter 8 to water and air travel.

The industrial history of roads is frequently neglected: this is regrettable, as there are many fascinating relics, both of the 'golden age of coaching' and the turnpike era, and indeed of more modern forms of transport, such as electric tramways.

Railway history has received rather more attention; it, too, can offer a fine heritage of buildings and engineering features, together with a certain amount of rolling stock preserved for posterity.

Road Transport

The history of Britain's roads dates from prehistoric times and many ancient trackways have been identified. The Roman period of occupation left a legacy of roads, many of which survive and are marked on Ordnance Survey maps. After the departure of the Romans, as a result of various factors road-building and maintenance declined but, with virtually no vehicular traffic, this caused little concern for hundreds of years.

In the 16th century inland travel increased, and this revealed the intolerable condition of the country's roads. An Act of Parliament was passed in 1555, making government responsible for organising the 'amending of highways being now very noisome and tedious to travel in and dangerous to all passengers and carriages'.[1] Although this historic Act remained in force for almost three centuries, it can hardly be described as effective. The Statute's basic weakness lay in that, under its provisions, responsibility was devolved to parish authorities. In the majority of cases, for various reasons, little was done to implement or enforce the Act.

By the mid-17th century, it was obvious that the increase in the volume of trade and the growth of industry were placing considerable pressure on England's transport resources, and that something would have to be done about the roads. They were in such an appalling condition that for much of the year even many main highways were impassable. Even when travel was possible, it was a slow and hazardous business, and certainly not to be undertaken for pleasure. Many roads were not suitable for wheeled vehicles, and this meant that many goods were carried by packhorse, which was very costly. The severity of the problem was not universal – some areas of the country fared much better than others – but the state of England's roads was generally placing a restraint on economic development.

The famous Turnpike Trust system evolved almost by accident. An Act of 1663 was passed 'for the repairing of highways within the counties of Hertford, Cambridge and Huntingdon', which comprised part of the old North Road, the major link between London and the North of England. Under the provisions of the Act, Justices of the Peace were able to levy tolls to pay for road maintenance: a measure regarded as both temporary and specific.[2] Its implementation met with so many problems that no similar legislation was passed for another 30 years, and even after that the system was initially adopted only very slowly.

Not surprisingly, the turnpike system, organised on the principle that those who used the roads most paid more towards their maintenance, was very unpopular. Sometimes disapproval was expressed by petitioning Parliament; often people took the law into their own hands. There were turnpike riots in many parts of the country, and the destruction of toll-gates was not uncommon. This unrest provoked a swift reaction: by 1727 the wilful destruction of toll-gates was punishable by three months' imprisonment and a public whipping. Later, sentences for such offences became even harsher.[3]

The turnpike trust system was eventually accepted, albeit grudgingly, and resulted in considerable improvements in conditions. By no means all roads were turnpiked, but by 1750 almost 1,400 miles of road had come under the system,[4] and by the end of the 18th century about 600 Turnpike Acts had been passed.[5] It is probably fair to suggest that, without it, the influence of the industrial revolution would have had a far slower effect.

Hampshire's first turnpike trust was the Petersfield and Sheet, for which the Act of Parliament was passed in 1711. Many other trusts followed, and by 1850 there were 37 in the county, covering more than 700 miles of highway.[6] The Isle of Wight did not have turnpikes, but its Highways Board, set up in 1813, was organised in much the same manner, and the road transport heritage of the mainland and the island are similar.

The so-called 'golden age' of coaching lasted from about 1820 until the early 1840s, made possible by the road improvements under the turnpike system. This was the era of coaching inns, providing not only rest and refreshment for the traveller, but offering many other facilities, such as stabling and care for horses, collection and distribution of mail, and in some instances they were used as meeting places (especially for the turnpike trusts!), as auction rooms, and even rudimentary banks.

Once the railway system became established, main road traffic declined, and by the latter part of the 19th century local authorities took over responsibility for road maintenance, and 'de-turnpiking' took place. Despite efforts to compete, the coaches could not match the service of the railways and, until the development of the internal combustion engine, rail triumphed over road.

Milestones are probably the most common and most easily seen relics of the turnpike trust and coaching days. Despite being removed or buried during the Second World War, many have been restored, and it is interesting to follow a former turnpike, checking how many survive. A particularly good set is on the 'old road' between Southampton and Winchester; this was the Southampton Turnpike, North and South Districts of 1757, and the set of milestones is complete. The stones are of conventional design, some now only inscribed, others retaining their cast iron plates. (Examples can be seen at SU 423179, SU 436208 and SU 467250.) Another road where milestone survival rate is fairly good is the A32, between the Hampshire/Berkshire county boundary, and Gosport. This was covered in the turnpike era by two trusts: the Basingstoke, Odiham and Alton (1736), and the Gosport, Bishops Waltham, Wickham and Chawton (1757/8). Some of these stones are inscribed, but many have cast iron plates. That not all these plates are original can be shown by closer inspection: a number bear the cast mark 'Wheatley 1891' (for example at SU 576106 on Hoads Hill, Wickham). In the late 1960s, Southampton University Industrial Archaeology Group carried out a survey of the industrial archaeology of the roads in the county and their findings were published.[7] This work, it must be remembered, was undertaken almost twenty years ago, but recent checks have shown that the majority of relics then recorded survive today.[8] It is particularly useful for 'milestone-spotting'.

Another feature of the turnpike age is the tollhouse; Hampshire is less rich in these than many counties, because early road widening schemes resulted in their demolition.

66. Milestone at Wickham.

Nevertheless, a number still survive, both purpose-built structures, and buildings in a suitable position which were used as tollhouses, though they pre-date the turnpike age. An example of the latter is at Lyndhurst (SU 298086), where a timber-framed building beside the present A337 is recorded as being used as a tollhouse. Of purpose-built tollhouses, a variety of designs can be seen in Hampshire. For instance, at Chineham, in the north, the tollhouse on the A33 (Reading and Basingstoke Turnpike, 1801) is a two-storey octagonal building with a central chimney (SU 666552). Although it has undergone major alterations, features identifying its former use include the recess for the toll-board above the blocked-in door on the side facing the road. A fine tollhouse, which has been in no way spoilt by its extensions, is that on the A31 (Winchester and Alton Turnpike, 1753), on the edge of New Alresford (SU 578324). A later example is that at Romsey (SU 360211), a single storey building dating from 1864. At this time, the turnpike was re-routed to avoid passing through the grounds of Broadlands, and thus a new tollhouse was required. A final example is a replacement, dating from c.1840, at Botley (SU 509137). This was erected at railway expense when the new railway caused the Lower St. Cross, Mill Lane to Park Gate Turnpike of 1810 to be diverted.

Coaching inns played an important role in the first half of the 19th century. Many survive, some greatly altered, some retaining original features. *The Star* in Southampton (SU 420115) still has its notice which advises of daily coaches to London, and mentions that the journey took ten hours. Others include a typical small coaching inn, *The King's Head*, in Wickham Square (SU 573115), and *The White Horse* at Romsey (SU 354212). The latter was a well known coaching inn during the 18th and 19th centuries, on the route between Southampton, Salisbury and Bath, and once had a cockpit under what is now the bar.

Examples of both milestones and tollhouses are to be found on the Isle of Wight. At Brighstone a rectangular milestone with a curved top, clearly inscribed, is set into a wall (SZ 428827). Other stones can be seen, all of similar design, at Blythe Shute, Blackgang (SZ 486772) and Shorwell (SZ 457830). The island has some very attractive tollhouses: at St. Lawrence (SZ 531764), an octagonal building on the A3055 of stone with a slate roof and iron window frames, served this purpose. At Hulverstone (SZ 401839), the single storey tollhouse is unusual, having a cross shaped ground plan. Other examples may be seen at Fairlee, Newport (SZ 511908), an octagonal brick building, and at Afton (SZ 356865).

There are a number of historic bridges in the county. Anjou, or Stony, Bridge at Titchfield (SU 543065) is of 17th-century date, replacing an earlier structure. Built of stone, with two arches, it has cutwaters carried to the parapet which act as passing places. One of the most complex bridge sites is that at Redbridge (SU 369137), on the outskirts of Southampton, where four road bridges cross the River Test. Until 1931, the main road was carried by a five-arch, 17th-century bridge connected by a causeway to a single span added in 1793. In

67. Tollhouse in Botley.

68. The *King's Head* coaching inn at Wickham

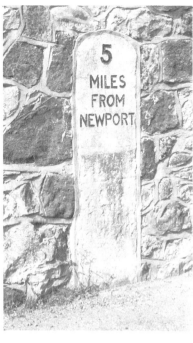

69. Milestone at Shorwell, Isle of Wight.

70. Tollhouse, St Lawrence, Isle of Wight.

71. Tollhouse, Hulverstone, Isle of Wight.

1931, they were replaced for traffic purposes by a concrete span, further downstream, which later was itself paralleled by a second concrete bridge.

Some of Hampshire's road bridges include attractive ironwork in their construction. One such is Norris's Bridge, Twyford (SU 476247), cast in 1891 to replace a 1750 road bridge across the River Itchen. At Upper Clatford (SU 357435), there is a very lovely iron bridge made in Taskers' foundry not far away. Dating from 1843, it consists of two cast iron arches, with perforated discs in the spandrels formed by their shallow curves. The handrails are held in place by iron columns.

On the Isle of Wight, a particularly noteworthy bridge can be seen at Grange Chine (SZ 422820). It is a mid-19th century, seven arch, red brick viaduct of the type used for railways, but which instead carried a two-lane road.

Other miscellaneous items include a cast iron marker on the county boundary between Hampshire and Berkshire (SU 724630). One toll road remains (SU 365125), crossing the causeway by Eling Mill. Although tolls are collected now on behalf of the New Forest District Council, until relatively recently the miller doubled as tollkeeper for the then owners, Winchester College. Towards the edge of Portsmouth (SU 654032), an obelisk, dating from 1799, marks the position of the town boundary at that time. At Shawford (SU 473250), until a few years ago, there was a small cabman's shelter opposite the entrance to the railway station. Although the building has now been demolished, and the site is overgrown, an area of granite sett still marks the position, a remarkable survival.

Many people will not regard the traditional 'finger' direction post as part of history; but it is rapidly disappearing, especially in urban areas, to be replaced by enamel signs. Occasionally they can still be found, as at the junction of Old Turnpike, Park Lane, Kiln Road and North Hill in Fareham (SU 575074). An enigmatic rural fingerpost is at Stephens Castle Down (SU 558215): one arm bears the inscription 'Upham $1\frac{1}{4}$' on one side, and 'Upham $1\frac{1}{2}$' on the other!

72. Finger post at Fareham.

Tramways

Within the present boundaries of the county of Hampshire four standard gauge electric tramway systems once operated: in the cities of Portsmouth and Southampton, a service between Gosport and Fareham, and the Portsdown and Horndean Light Railway. With the exception of the last, all were conventional street tramways, and had been preceded by horse-drawn trams. Public transport in Portsmouth began in 1840, when a horse bus service connected Southsea and North End.[9] Twenty-five years later the first horse trams ran in the city, and a network of routes gradually evolved until 1892 when 58 cars and 249 horses operated over 14 route miles.[10]

Almost all the tramways in Portsmouth were empowered under the 1870 Tramways Act, which allowed local authorities to acquire routes after 21 years. In the 1890s, the Corporation became increasingly involved and decided to take over the tramways, and to proceed with a change from horse to electric power. In 1901 Portsmouth's tramways were electrified and they continued in use until 1936 when trams were replaced by trolleybuses. A few relics of Portsmouth trams can still be found, including a length of sett-paved tram

73. Tram track, Rugby Road, Southsea.

74. Former tram shelter, Southsea.

track in Rugby Road, Southsea (SZ 650998), together with a former traction pole,[11] as well
as tramcar No. 84 in store at Eastney Bus Depot.[12] Some other items have been re-used: a
tramshelter in Southsea (SZ 638992), an attractive iron-framed structure, now gives shelter
to bus passengers. Similarly, a number of former traction poles, having been re-used by
trolleybuses, are now lamp standards (as at SU 652025).

Horse trams in Southampton first ran in 1879 where, like Portsmouth, they were preceded
by horse bus services.[13] By 1896 the service covered about 400,000 miles annually,[14] having
grown steadily despite various financial and other problems.

In 1898 the Southampton trams passed into municipal ownership and two years later the
first section of the system was electrified. The city's tram service had a longer life than
Portsmouth's: trams were replaced by diesel buses as part of post-war planning, and the
last tram ran on 31 December 1949. The heritage of Southampton's tramways is limited to
a number of traction poles re-used for street lighting. There is a fine set in Lodge Road (SU
420153-426136) with ornamental cast iron bases. However, several of the tramcars are being
preserved. Car No. 45 is part of the collection at Crich Tramway Museum, Derbyshire, and
the 'Tram 57' Group have for some years been working on the restoration of former
Southampton tramcars. Car No. 11 is now almost completely restored to working order,
and a great deal has been achieved on Car No. 38.

Gosport's horse trams came into use in 1882, but were never taken over by the corporation.
They were run by the Gosport Street Tramways Company, a subsidiary of the Provincial
Tramways Company; when motor buses replaced trams, the company retained the name
'Provincial'. The system was electrified in 1905, and in the same year was extended to
Fareham; the service continued until 1929 when the buses took over. A lone traction pole,
which doubles as a stench pipe (see Chapter 6), can be seen on the outskirts of Fareham
(SU 573063); otherwise the only archaeological evidence is the tram track buried beneath
the road, which is revealed by roadworks.

The fourth of the local tramway companies differed from the others. The Hampshire
Light Railways (Electric) Company Ltd. (a subsidiary of Provincial Tramways) was
incorporated in 1897. This in turn became the Portsdown and Horndean Light Railway
Company, which ran an electric tramway service between Cosham and Horndean – in some
places beside the road, in others on the road itself like conventional tramways – from 1903
until 1935. It was then bought out by Southdown Motor Services who were already running
buses along the route. The fragmentary remains of this enterprise are a traction pole (SU
669067) near the *George* public house, and the abutments of a bridge which crossed Southwick
Hill Road (SU 658058) near Queen Alexandra Hospital.

The only tramway to run on the Isle of Wight was in Ryde. From 1871 horse trams ran
from Ryde Pier Head to the original terminus of the railway at St. John's Road (SZ 596919).
In 1880 the train service from the Pier Head opened, and only the section of the tramway
on the pier remained in use. It transferred to electric power in 1886 and later there were
unsuccessful experiments with steam.[15] In the 1920s petrol-driven railcars were introduced,
and these ran until the tramway was finally closed in 1969.

Railways

A vast amount has been written about almost every aspect of railway history, so in this
book only a brief summary will be given, with examples of some of the rich heritage which
can be seen. The bibliography (Appendix 1) suggests some more specialised books on the
subject.

The Act which authorised the building of the first railway in Hampshire was passed in
1834.[16] This was the London to Southampton line, completed in 1840, with a branch line

75. Southampton Terminus Station.

76. Gosport Station.

to Gosport via Fareham being added in 1842.[17] This was of particular significance since, until 1847, the terminus at Gosport was the station serving Portsmouth.[18]

Three particular railway developments occurred in 1847, one being the opening of the line to Portsmouth (to the station now known as Portsmouth and Southsea).[19] Secondly, the London and South Western Railway opened a branch line from what was then Bishopstoke (later re-named Eastleigh) to Salisbury. Finally, the Southampton and Dorchester railway, with a line running from a junction half a mile north of Southampton Terminus station via Ringwood and Wareham to Dorchester, was opened.

Of these early developments quite substantial remains can be seen. Although Southampton's Central Station has undergone rebuilding and nothing of the original survives, the magnificent Terminus station building can be seen (SU 426111). Its platforms have gone and its interior has been altered; recently, after years of neglect, it has been restored for use as a night-club. It was designed by Sir William Tite, who was also the architect responsible for Gosport Station, Winchester Station and the original building, on the upside, at Eastleigh. His design at Gosport was a particularly interesting one: to avoid interfering with the town's defences, he planned a long low building with an elaborate colonnade. The station suffered war damage and was never fully restored. After the line closed to passengers in 1953 and to freight in 1969, the station slipped gradually into dereliction and, despite efforts to find a new use for it, it is now a sad sight. The colonnade, however, survives, as do parts of the platforms and station buildings (SU 615002). The site's future is very uncertain.

Another station of this early period is that at Micheldever (SU 518428), which was built to serve Andover, and consequently, until 1856, was known as Andover Road; the station at Andover was opened in 1854. At Micheldever, the original building on the upside, with its canopy on all sides of the building, remains. Another feature is the use of flint in its construction, with yellow bricks at the corners, windows and doors, and stone for the sills and keystones of the windows.[20]

A major engineering work of 1848 survives at Fareham, where two viaducts, one of 11 arches, the other of 17, can be seen. One carries the railway between the town and the quay (SU 580059); the other crosses the main road to Portsmouth and the head of Fareham Creek (SU 587063). Both viaducts are still in use and little altered.

Another facet of railway heritage is the crossing keeper's cottage. Although most are now disused, many have survived in Hampshire as private homes. An interesting example is in Portsmouth (SU 660014), where the Copnor crossing was closed in 1908 and replaced by an overbridge, but the house remains, a building of stuccoed brick with ornamental lintels over the windows.

After the 1840s there was a steady growth in Hampshire's railway network, with many new lines, including a direct line to Portsmouth via Haslemere in 1859, and the works on this line included such stations as that at Petersfield (SU 743236), typical of its period with two asymmetrical high gables and characteristic windows. Nearby, a traditional signal box survives (SU 744236), though no longer in use.

The Mid-Hants. Railway, which was completed in 1865, has a most remarkable history. Closed by British Rail in 1973, despite considerable opposition, it was taken over by a group of enthusiasts who first re-opened the stretch between Alresford and Ropley in 1977, and now run regular steam trains from Alresford to Alton (see Appendix 2). Ropley Station (SU 630324) has won a number of preservation awards and, with its topiary and enamel advertising signs, has a wonderfully nostalgic air of the 'good old days of steam'.

A branch line of this period which is less well-known than most is that which ran from Botley to Bishop's Waltham. Although plans were laid to link it with both the Mid-Hants. and the Portsmouth direct line, neither of these proposals ever came to fruition. The Bishop's

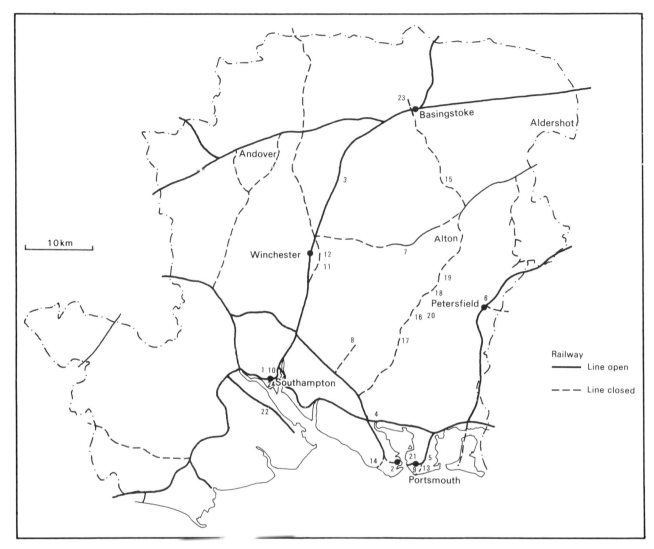

Map 4. Hampshire railways.

Waltham branch opened in 1863, carried passenger traffic until 1933, and finally closed to goods traffic in 1962. A newspaper account of the opening of the line paints a delightful picture of the occasion: 'The beautifully toned bells of the old parish church were ringing a merry peal the whole day, and a celebrated brass band paraded the town: the Bishop's Waltham Rifle Band also assisted'.[21] The line was used extensively for the movement of local pottery products (see Chapter 4). Now, like Blanchards, little remains of the Bishop's Waltham branch. Part of the line can be followed on foot; near the station site the remains of a level crossing gate can be seen (SU 549175). The station itself was demolished, and a large roundabout stands on the site.

Besides new developments, the mid-Victorian period was also a time of consolidation for Hampshire's railways. Portsmouth and Southsea station (SU 642003) was rebuilt in 1866 and with its ornamental ironwork is typical of its period. A decade later it was agreed at last that the railway could breach the fortifications of Portsmouth and the line was extended to Portsmouth Harbour station (SU 628001).

One of the finest buildings of the period is what is now South Western House, Southampton (SU 427111). This opened as the *Imperial Hotel* in 1869, but three years later was renamed the *South Western Hotel*, when it was taken over by the London and South Western Railway. It remained in use as an hotel, often patronised by those about to board the great liners, until the Second World War. It now has a number of tenants, including Cunard and the B.B.C. Although there has been major alteration to the interior, its marble-lined entrance hall survives among other features.

77. Hockley Viaduct.

The last two decades of the 19th century heralded yet more change to the local railway network. As mentioned in Chapter 5, Eastleigh developed as a railway town, and the London and South Western Railway lost its monopoly of Southampton traffic. In 1882 the Didcot, Newbury and Southampton railway was authorised to build a line from Newbury to Southampton, but it was never completed, and ended at Winchester. A link was built to the LSWR line at Shawford, which included the Hockley Railway Viaduct (SU 477266). This 33-arch structure is the longest railway viaduct in Hampshire and, although disused since the mid-1960s, at present survives, though its future has been in doubt on a number of occasions. Dating from 1891, it is a remarkable piece of engineering, being built of concrete with a chalk core, and covered by a brick skin. Of the DNSR terminus at Winchester, nothing remains except a tunnel next to the station site (SU 487294).

One short-lived venture was the East Southsea line in Portsmouth. It operated only from 1885 until 1914, but indications of its existence include part of the station (SZ 650984), its porte-cochère and concourse being preserved as part of a motor dealer's premises.

A number of features of late 19th-century and early 20th-century railways can still be seen, though the lines have been closed. The Lee-on-Solent railway was opened in 1894 from Fort Brockhurst; it last carried passengers in 1930 and freight in 1935, but the station is still used, as an amusement arcade (SU 564005). Two very contrasting lines, both dating from the beginning of this century and both long since closed, are the Basingstoke and Alton, opened by the LSWR in 1901, and the Meon Valley Railway of 1903. The Basingstoke and Alton was authorised under the Light Railways Act of 1896, being the first line to take advantage of these powers.[22] Its construction took as simple a form as possible, with cheap station buildings of corrugated iron. Bentworth and Lasham station is a good surviving example (SU 669417), and is now used as a coal depot.

On the other hand, the Meon Valley railway, for reasons which have never been explained, was built in impressive style. Far from being like the Basingstoke and Alton, a typical Edwardian light railway, the Meon Valley was provided with engineering works to take double track, an imposing viaduct, station platforms nearly 600 feet long, and elaborate station buildings.[23] At West Meon, for instance, the buildings were of red brick with stone surrounds to doors and windows; the fine gables had a Tudor air, and even the gentlemen's lavatories were far from merely functional: square detached buildings like Chinese pagodas.[24] As Dr. Course observes, the five original Meon Valley stations (Wickham, Droxford, West Meon, Tisted and Privett) probably represented some of the most costly stations per head of population to be found anywhere.[25] Three of these stations survive in good order as private houses: Droxford (SU 613187), Tisted (SU 707322) and Privett (SU 673286). The others gradually fell derelict and were demolished after the line closed, to passengers in 1955 and to goods in 1962. At West Meon, the once splendid station is hard to imagine, the site being heavily overgrown, and the only remains are small parts of the platform, obscured by the undergrowth. Of the impressive West Meon viaduct (SU 644240), only the massive concrete blocks which supported the metal piers remain; the four 56-foot steel spans have long been removed.

Recent decades have seen a considerable contraction of the county's railways, although all the main lines remain in use. The memory of the many lost branch lines evokes a deep feeling of nostalgia.[26] The decline of the railways on the Isle of Wight has been even more dramatic. Noting that the island was once served by no less than three railway companies, with 30 stations and more than 50 miles of track, it is hard to believe that this has been reduced to a handful of stations and just eight and a half miles of public railway, with a short stretch of preserved line.

The Isle of Wight's railway history begins with the opening of the line linking Cowes and Newport. This was part of the Isle of Wight Central Railway, which was later to cover a much greater part of the island. When this first stretch was opened, however, it seems to have caused little interest. Michael Robbins draws attention to an entry in the *Hampshire Telegraph and Sussex Chronicle*, which recorded that 'scarce half a dozen people' travelled by the first train on the morning of 16 June 1862.[27]

78. Horringford Station, Isle of Wight.

The next line to be opened was that of the Isle of Wight Railway, between St. John's Road, Ryde and Shanklin, in 1864, with an extension to Ventnor two years later. As already mentioned, a link from Ryde Pier to St. John's Road opened in 1880, being a joint venture by the LSWR and the LBSCR companies. It is the stretch from Ryde to Shanklin which is the only British Rail line to remain open on the island today. In the years that followed, the island's network grew, both through the two companies already mentioned and with the building of the Freshwater, Yarmouth and Newport Railway in the late 1880s, although this company was never very successful. For the first half of the 20th century, there was little real change; decline did not begin until the early 1950s, when the first lines closed – the 'Fresh', and minor branches. The main and dramatic change came in the 'Beeching' era, with major closures in 1966, just before the change from steam to electric traction.

Steam can still be seen on the Isle of Wight: preservationists run a service between Havenstreet and a point near the site of Wootton station. At Havenstreet Station (SZ 556898), a museum has been opened (see Appendix 2) and several locomotives and a quantity of rolling stock are preserved.

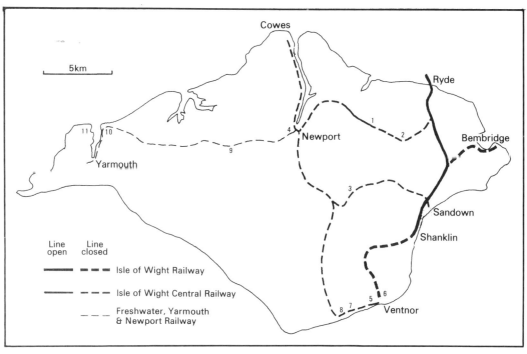

Map 5. Isle of Wight railways.

KEY

1. Havenstreet station
2. Ashey station
3. Horringford station
4. 'Fresh' offices, Newport
5. Ventnor West station
6. Ventnor tunnel
7. St Lawrence station
8. St Lawrence tunnel
9. Watchingwell station
10. Yarmouth station
11. Fort Victoria -- narrow gauge track

Despite the dramatic contraction of the Isle of Wight's railways, their heritage is remarkable. Of the stations, the majority survive, frequently re-used as houses. Good examples include Horringford (SZ 543854), Ashey (SZ 578889), Yarmouth (SZ 357894), St. Lawrence (SZ 534766), Ventnor West (SZ 553773) and Watchingwell (SZ 448884). This last is of particular interest, as it was a private station built for the Simeon family of Swainston. Of the other features, the tunnel at St. Lawrence (SZ 527768-531765) was the largest engineering undertaking by the Isle of Wight Central Railway, and is 619 yards long. Both portals can be seen; the north end of the tunnel is used for growing mushrooms. At Ventnor, although the main station has been obliterated by an industrial estate, the tunnel which carried the railway under St. Boniface Down remains, still housing water pipes. Its southern portal can be seen from the estate (at SZ 561780). It had originally been intended to run the railway between Sandown and Ventnor via Luccombe and Bonchurch, but opposition by Lord Yarborough, a local landowner, resulted instead in the 1,312-yard long tunnel.[28]

Another relic of the island's railway history is the former office building of the Freshwater, Yarmouth and Newport railway. This was a corrugated iron hut which still stands opposite Towngate Mill, Newport (SZ 497895). A study of the remains of the island's railways can be very interesting: the bibliography in Appendix 1 offers suggestions for further reading.

Private Railways

In recent times many private railways have been closed and then obliterated. Many of those in Hampshire and the one on the Isle of Wight were associated with the armed forces;

79. Signal, Dockyard branch, Edinburgh Road, Portsmouth.

80. Narrow-gauge track, Fort Victoria, Isle of Wight.

Portsmouth Dockyard once had a railway system of some 35 miles of track, but this has been closed for some years, and much of the track now lies beneath tarmac. On the old link between the Dockyard and Portsmouth and Southsea High Level Station, two sets of level crossing gates can be seen at Alfred Road (SU 639006) and at Edinburgh Road (SU 640005), and until recently a remarkable survival was a double armed wooden semaphore signal at the Edinburgh Road crossing. This has now been dismantled and is to be preserved by Portsmouth City Museums. Other survivals include that at Marchwood (SU 395104), where the Army have an extensive railway system, and on the Isle of Wight at Fort Victoria (SZ 340898), where a small section of narrow gauge track laid in the 1850s can be seen.

It was once commonplace for large mental hospitals to have their own railway systems, which often connected to the main line. Of the one at Park Prewett, the station building (SU 615540), a platform and a weighbridge survive.

From Hythe Pier (SU 423081), a regular ferry service runs to Southampton (see Chapter 8). The pier railway of two-foot gauge conveys passengers to the pier head, on third-rail electrified track, and it also carries supplies of fuel oil for the ferries.

Chapter Eight

Transport II: Water and Air

Water Transport
Inland navigation was never as important in Hampshire as in the land-locked Midlands and the North; indeed, on the Isle of Wight no canals were specially built. Their long coastlines, however, encouraged considerable maritime activity.

Inland Waterways
Although neither very important to the county's economy, nor particularly successful, a few canals were built in Hampshire, although in some cases only slight traces of their existence are to be found.

81. Andover Canal, Romsey.

The Andover Canal, which ran between Redbridge, on the edge of Southampton, and the centre of Andover had a fairly short life, being opened in 1794 and closed in 1857. There had been a proposal for a Test Navigation in the late 17th century, which would have linked Romsey and Southampton, but this was abandoned, and in 1789 an Act of Parliament was passed enabling the cut to be made which would become the Andover Canal. The Act was unusually detailed, even stipulating the hours between which vessels could pass along the 22 miles of waterway. Like all Hampshire canals, the Andover Canal was always a disappointment to its promoters. It was mainly used to carry agricultural produce to Southampton, and to bring supplies of coal, stone and the like inland,[1] but this was insufficient to sustain its financial viability, and when it closed in 1857 the proprietors formed the Andover Canal Railway Company, later the Andover and Redbridge Railway. Parts of the canal bed were used by the railway; at Romsey, though, a stretch still contains water, and both canal and towpath are clearly defined at the point where they pass under the railway line to Salisbury (SU 358215). Other stretches can be discerned, although often with difficulty, but at Redbridge (SU 371138) a building survives, much altered,which once served as a warehouse for the canal company.

Another inland waterway noted mainly for its lack of success – indeed it was never completed – was the Southampton and Salisbury Canal, which consisted of two arms linked by the Andover Canal. The eastern, Southampton, arm started at Redbridge and was intended to join the sea. In the western direction, the waterway was to run from a junction with the Andover Canal at Kimbridge and go west to Salisbury. Neither arm was finished; the eastern arm was dogged with difficulties, in particular the necessity for a tunnel passing under Southampton, and in the west work never progressed beyond Alderbury.

The Canal's authorising Act was passed in 1795, and at the point of its maximum development, c.1804, navigation was possible between Alderbury and the western end of Southampton. After this, the story was one of decline. As early as February 1805 it was stated that 'The Southampton and Salisbury canal is not going on at all at present, but rather backwards as the works are going very fast to Decay'.[2] Parts of the canal remained in intermittent use, but gradually all traffic ceased. The waterway has left only scant remains; most of it has been obliterated. Near Lockerley, it is possible to see the remains of Lock No.4 (SU 289268) from the road between Holbury Wood and Lockerley Green, but the most significant survival is one which cannot be seen – the canal tunnel under the City of Southampton. Evidence suggests that this was never fully navigable, but it has certainly posed engineering difficulties at intervals since its construction. In the 1840s there was a scheme to take the line of the Southampton and Dorchester railway through the tunnel, but it was soon decided that its poor condition would render this impossible, and a line cutting across the tunnel was chosen instead.[3] Falls of earth created problems and, well over a century later in the 1970s, part of the tunnel collapsed, causing subsidence of the ground above. At this time an investigation of the tunnel was made and a full record compiled.[4]

Yet another waterway which was a failure was the Portsea Island Canal, which ran between Langstone Harbour and a terminal basin in the centre of Portsmouth (at what is now the junction of Commercial Road with Arundel Street). The project was to be part of the Portsmouth and Arundel Canal, but after its opening in 1822 it never attracted much trade, and complaints were received that leakage of sea water was contaminating the drinking supply of the town.[5] By 1827, the canal's short life was over and it had been drained.[6] Its eastern end does retain some traces; the sea lock at Langstone (SZ 678999) survives, although in rather poor condition, and a former beam engine pumping house, used to maintain the level of water, can be seen in Waterlock Gardens (SZ 675998). Further west, roads and the railway made use of the canal bed, but odd reminders can be seen, such as traces of the hawthorn hedge that lined the southern bank.[7]

Three Hampshire waterways predated the canal period. Of the Avon Navigation linking Salisbury and Christchurch some remains of artificial cuts on its course may be seen. The Titchfield Canal, too, was of 17th-century date, promoted by Henry, Earl of Southampton. Traces of this waterway are scarce, but part of the masonry of the sea lock (SU 531027), which is now cut off from the sea by defence works, is still visible from a road bridge.

Of the third of the early waterways, the Itchen Navigation, much more remains, and it is possible to walk the 10¾ miles of this with only minor diversions. Much of its length no longer contains water, but the walk is a pleasant one, not only for the canal features, but also for the wildlife and plants. Although improvements to the River Itchen had been made as early as the 12th century, the works surviving today date from the passing of an Act in 1665 which specified that the river should be 'Made Navigable and Passable for Boats, Barges and other vessels'.[8] By 1710, after various delays, the river with artificial cuts was navigable from Woodmill, Southampton to Blackbridge Wharf, Winchester. Its story is an interesting and complex one,[9] but like other Hampshire waterways it was never very successful

82. Site of wheel pit, Catherine Hill Lock, Itchen Navigation.

and, by about 1870, commercial traffic had finally ceased. The Itchen Navigation had finally been defeated by railway competition but, even as early as the 1720s, Defoe had observed that the navigation had 'never answer'd the expence, so as to give encouragement to the undertakers'.[10] Remains of a number of the navigation's 15 locks survive, together with other features. For example, at Catherine Hill Lock, the summit lock of the waterway (SU 480274), the lock chamber is still clearly visible, with a weir and sluice roughly in the position of the upper gates. Also to be seen is the wheel pit, where a waterwheel once powered a sawmill next to the lock. Conegar Lock (SU 466188) is typical of the turf-sided locks on the Itchen Navigation, although a brick toe was put in to prevent erosion. There is also a set of hatches at the head of the lock, used for drowning watermeadows (see Chapter 2). Mansbridge, Southampton (SU 448155) dates from 1816 and, although now only for pedestrians, once carried a major road over the navigation.

The Basingstoke Canal was in some respects the most successful of the county's inland waterways, although it too failed to meet the expectations of its promoters. Opened in 1794 to link the town with the River Wey, and thence London, its net revenue was seldom more than £2,000, just over a quarter of what was anticipated.[11] After a chequered and rather sad history, commercial traffic on the Hampshire section of the canal ceased in the early years of the 20th century. In recent years, however, it has undergone restoration. The terminus at Basingstoke has long since disappeared under modern development, but a length of the Hampshire part of the canal – as far as the Greywell Tunnel (SU 708518-719515) – is navigable, and public boat trips are run. A number of sites remain identifiable, including Ash Lock (SU 881518), the only one of the canal's 29 locks to be found in Hampshire. This has now been fully restored. A detailed account of the canal's fascinating history is available (see Appendix 1).

Southampton Docks

The protected nature of Southampton Water, and the famous phenomenon of the double tide, has provided Southampton with geographical advantages which make it a natural port. This it has been for centuries, enjoying particular prosperity during the Middle Ages through the wool and wine trades. It then suffered a decline; as Daniel Defoe wrote in the 18th century, 'the decay of the trade is the real decay of the town; and all the business of moment that is transacted there, is the trade between us and the islands of Jersey and Guernsey, with a little of the wine trade'.[12] In the early part of the last century, however, its natural assets were fully appreciated, and an Act of Parliament was passed in 1803, authorising the creation of docks, warehouses and piers. The Southampton Dock Company was formed in 1836, and two years later the foundation stone of the first dock was laid. This stone has now been removed and is preserved on a plinth, not far from the main entrance to the Eastern Docks (SU 425106).

In 1842 the company opened its first dock, the Outer or Princess Alexandra Dock (SU 430108). This has been greatly altered, but can still be seen as a feature of the Ocean Village development which now occupies part of the Eastern Docks. From the 1840s until well into this century the dock complex grew steadily. In 1892 it was taken over by the London and South Western Railway, and the investment made by them resulted in Southampton by the first decade of the 20th century, becoming the United Kingdom's premier passenger port; by 1930, it was dealing with more than half a million passengers a year. At that time, managed and owned by the Southern Railway, the docks covered some 200 acres and, besides the passenger traffic, were handling an ever increasing volume of freight.[13] As well as the Outer Dock, vessels could now use the Inner Dock (1851), the Empress Dock (1890), and the Ocean Dock (1912). The ships of the famous shipping lines – Cunard's *Aquitania* and *Mauretania* and later the 'Queens', White Star's *Oceanic*, *Olympic* and the ill-fated *Titanic*, and Union Castle's *Edinburgh Castle* and *Dunluce Castle* – all sailed from Southampton. They were served by boat trains; the railway network in the Eastern Docks was extensive. Dry docks were constructed for the repair and maintenance of vessels.

Between 1929 and 1934, the Western Docks were developed on more than 400 acres of reclaimed land with 8,000 feet of quay, and a dry dock. As the port's passenger traffic has steadily declined in recent decades, with travel by air rendering the great liners redundant, it has been replaced by more freight traffic. The most important recent development in the Docks is the Prince Charles Container Terminal, a sophisticated modern complex which now houses the Port of Southampton's main area of activity.

Nationalisation of the railway network in 1948 resulted in the transfer of docks ownership to the British Transport Commission.[14] This was superceded in 1963 by the British Transport Docks Board[15] and, in 1982, privatisation led to the managing body becoming known as Associated British Ports.[16]

In recent years the Eastern Docks have undergone dramatic change. The Inner Dock and all but one of the dry docks have been filled in; the Ocean Terminal, opened in 1950 to serve passengers disembarking from ships in Ocean Dock, was demolished in 1983. The one surviving dry dock is No.6, the Trafalgar Dry Dock of 1905 (SU 422105); this was altered after completion to facilitate its use by the S.S. *Berengaria* (formerly the German *Imperateur*, part of First World War reparations). The Ocean Dock itself survives (SU 424105), with massive grain silos on one side reflecting the change in the traffic using it. The Empress Dock (SU 425102) opened by Queen Victoria can also be seen. The facade of the former Continental Booking Office (SU 428109) has been incorporated into Ocean Village, but little else of note survives, except for a solitary warehouse (SU 426108).

Quays and Piers
Coastal trade over the centuries, has been very important both to Hampshire and to the Isle of Wight. In rare cases, like Lepe (SZ 432988), a quay was constructed specifically to

export a local product, in this instance bricks; usually quays and landing places dealt with a wide variety of commodities including coal, timber and grain. In their heyday in the 18th and 19th centuries, these minor ports bustled with traffic; today their use is normally confined to pleasure craft, although some exceptions survive. Many landing places, like Lymington and Gosport, have been transformed with little to show of their commercial past. Emsworth has also undergone redevelopment, but retains some reminders of the past, such as the rendered warehouse by Quay Mill pond (SU 748055).[17] An exception to the paucity of heritage in small ports is Fareham (SU 579057), which still has some minor commercial traffic, mostly sand and ballast dredged from the Solent. Besides the former ropewalk (see Chapter 3) and the electricity generating station (Chapter 6), there is the block of flats (SU 579058) which was from 1830 until 1960 a steam flour mill, after which it was used by various industrial concerns until its recent conversion. Also on the quay is an attractive 18th-century warehouse (SU 579055), distinctive with its wooden-framed unglazed windows.

A site still in use for commercial traffic, but with relatively little in the way of historic relics, is the Camber Dock, Portsmouth (SZ 631995). This, the original landing place for the town, has been much altered, and little remains besides some 19th-century bollards and fragments of earlier walls.

On the Isle of Wight, many former landing places and quays have suffered a fate similar to those on the mainland. Brading Quay (SZ 614873) has virtually disappeared. Disused for more than a century, when an embankment was built in the 1870s between Bembridge and St. Helens and the marshes were drained, it is just possible to discern what was the edge of the old quay under considerable undergrowth. Newtown was once important as a port, but larger vessels and heavy silting of the estuary resulted in its gradual abandonment. Now one small storehouse and a short stretch of quay are all that survive (SZ 419912).[18] At Shalfleet, on the other hand, the quay is still used by pleasure craft (SZ 414904), and a former coal store can be seen.

Newport was a major port from the Middle Ages, but recently has considerably changed its character. Many warehouses have been converted (one is an Arts Centre), but other features include the unusual hand crane with a parasol top which stands on the quay (SZ 501896), next to a three-storey brick building which has hoists on both sides. Its former ownership is indicated by the legend near the roof line, 'British Road Services'. On the other side of the river, another warehouse can be seen (SZ 501895), bearing a datestone of 1895. This brick building, three storeys high, has hoist gantries protruding over the water, and a small wall crane on one corner.

A number of piers are to be found, both in Hampshire and on the Isle of Wight. Most have been used for transport and for pleasure and, of those which remain, some are still in use, despite the high cost of upkeep.

Both Portsmouth's piers are relatively modern, although replacements of earlier structures. The original Clarence Pier, 80 yards in length, opened in 1861, and had a horse tram connection with the Town Station until 1876. The pier was almost completely destroyed by enemy action in 1941, and the present structure (SZ 635988) dates from the 1960s. To the west, South Parade Pier has also had its share of misfortune. A pier of 400 yards long, principally constructed to attract ferry traffic for the Isle of Wight, was built in 1879. This was destroyed by fire in 1904 and, four years later, its replacement, 608 feet long, was completed, but that too suffered a fire in the early 1970s when the pier was being used as a film set. The buildings were virtually destroyed, and repair work was undertaken to restore the pier to use (SZ 652980). In the Southampton area two piers can be seen. Hythe Pier (SU 425085), built in 1880, is still used regularly; a ferry crosses from there to Southampton. It is over 2,000 feet long and its pierhead buildings retain their Victorian

83.   Fareham quay.

84.   Warehouse, Fareham quay.

character. Passage along the pier can be taken by narrow gauge railway (see Chapter 7). Southampton's Royal Pier (SU 418109) has lost its transport function and now only the entrance buildings are in use, as a restaurant. In its heyday this was one of the busiest piers on the south coast, used by both commercial and pleasure traffic. Most of the pier itself was destroyed by fire in 1987.

Several of the piers on the Isle of Wight have also suffered from damage, repairs and extensions. Six examples survive, three of which have been primarily used only for landing places; the others were also venues for entertainment. At Yarmouth (SZ 354898), the 700-foot pier has recently undergone restoration, while that at Totland Bay (SZ 323872), built in 1870, has very little to offer in the way of facilities. The third of the piers dedicated almost solely to transport, and the most important, is that at Ryde (SZ 594929). The original pier on the site was 1,250 feet long, and built in wood in 1813-14.[19] Alterations and extensions were made in 1824 and 1833, lengthening the pier by 1,000 feet. It is still in use, with three separate tracks: the railway (see Chapter 7), the pedestrian deck which incorporates the original structure and, in the centre, a disused tramway.

At Sandown, Shanklin and Ventnor the piers, as befits such resorts, were designed for entertainment as well as transport needs. That at Sandown (SZ 598840) has been much altered, and now houses a large entertainment complex. Shanklin Pier (SZ 586814), built in 1891, was 1,200 feet long, with its concert pavilion having been rebuilt after a fire in 1927; unfortunately much of the pier was destroyed in the hurricane which battered the island in October 1987. Finally, Ventnor Pier (SZ 563773) (of special interest to the author as her paternal grandfather was its piermaster for a time shortly after the First World War) has had a chequered history, and its future is far from secure. Dating from 1872, it sustained damage in the Second World War and was substantially rebuilt in the 1950s. More recently it became unsafe, and a fire has left it under threat of demolition.

One final aspect of maritime traffic which must be mentioned is the floating bridges. These at one time existed in three locations in the area, but only one survives. A chain ferry linked Portsmouth and Gosport from the early Victorian period until 1958; almost no evidence remains of this. Southampton and Woolston were similarly linked from 1836 till 1977. This service too has been almost obliterated, save for the shell of No. 11 Floating Bridge which was converted into a nightclub, and stands beside the former landing stage at Woolston (SU 435112). It was badly damaged by fire in 1987. The history of the Southampton Floating Bridge has been recorded (see Appendix 1).

On the Isle of Wight, however, a floating bridge still runs between East and West Cowes (SZ 500956-502955). Although the craft used today are modern, the service across the River Medina has operated since 1859.

Air Transport

The Solent area was one of the cradles of the aircraft industry, with several airfields active before the First World War, and both aeroplanes and seaplanes have been manufactured in Hampshire and on the Isle of Wight.

On 16 October 1908 Samuel F. Cody made the first official flight in the British Isles, from the Army's Balloon Factory and School at Farnborough (SU 869545). This spurred on aeronautical activity and, by 1909, flying was pioneered in various parts of Hampshire. Geoffrey de Havilland used a field at Seven Barrows, to the north of Whitchurch, where a commemorative stone now stands (SU 463561).[20] Beaulieu Airfield (SU 372006) came into use in 1910, and the New Forest Flying School was run there for about 18 months. The aerodrome was re-opened by the Royal Flying Corps from 1915 until 1919.[21] It was used sporadically until the Second World War when a new larger airfield was opened about a mile to the west (SU 350005), which was used for the duration of the war and for a short

85. Cowes floating bridge, Isle of Wight.

time afterwards, when it housed the Airborne Forces Experimental Establishment.[22] Little of note survives on either site.

Other bases, including that for seaplanes at Calshot,were opened just before and during the First World War but, on the cessation of hostilities, many military airfields were abandoned and the land returned to agricultural use. Some sites remained operational, for example at Worthy Down (SU 470350) and at Andover (SU 330455). Although the grass airfield was closed in 1980, Andover is still the best preserved First World War airfield in the county. It retains some of its hangars, with wooden Belfast-truss roofs and brick buttresses.

On the civilian side, the inter-war years were a time of development. After the departure of the Americans from Eastleigh (SU 450170) (see Chapter 5) in April 1919, the buildings were used for some time as a transit camp for European immigrants to the United States of America. In 1932, the airfield was opened by Southampton Corporation as a municipal airport and, apart from the duration of the Second World War, it has remained a civilian aerodrome ever since, although it is now in private hands. Some early hangars survive, a number of which are now used by the Ford Motor Company whose premises adjoin the aerodrome.[23] A civilian airport was also opened to serve Portsmouth, built on reclaimed land on the shore of Langstone Harbour. Portsmouth Airport was closed some years ago, and the site (SU 670035) is now covered by an industrial estate and houses.

The threat of the Second World War resulted in a flurry of military aeronautical activity. At Lee-on-Solent, the Royal Naval Air Service had had a training station for seaplane

86. Terminal buildings, Portsmouth Airport.

87. Former hangar at Apse Manor near Sandown on the Isle of Wight.

pilots since 1917. In 1937, they opened an aerodrome which was substantially extended during the war when hard runways were laid down (SU 560020). Another important site at this time was near Stockbridge. The Royal Flying Corps operated between 1917 and 1919 from an airfield at Houghton Down (SU 333353). Between 1940 and 1945, however, a second airstrip on the west side of the road to Danebury Hill was used by Vickers Armstrong Ltd. for testing Spitfires. In the woods (SU 330362) were the assembly sheds, but little archaeological evidence survives.[24]

Another pre-war development was at Odiham, where an R.A.F. station was built in 1937 (SU 740490). Most of the original buildings survive, and the station is still operational; it is an excellent example of an R.A.F. station of its period.[25] Other survivals include hangars at Titchfield (SU 530070), now part of the Plessey Works, but built in 1935 as the local base for the Southampton anti-aircraft balloon barrage, and at Lasham, where three T2 hangars dating from the 1940s remain as relics of a typical standard operational R.A.F. airfield.

Sites of seaplane manufacture are mentioned in Chapter 5. Besides being used by the armed forces and for scheduled civilian flights, these craft were a common sight between the wars in the Solent area, in the heyday of the Schneider Trophy Races which were held locally on many occasions. On 13 September 1931, off Calshot, Britain took the trophy for the third successive time, and this made the country outright winners. In Appendix 1 are listed some useful books on this subject.

On the Isle of Wight a former hangar, used during the First World War at Bembridge as part of a seaplane base, has been moved to Shanklin, where it is now used as an amusement arcade (SZ 586815). At Bembridge itself, most of the present buildings are modern, although some older ones can be seen (SZ 632869). The role of this airfield in the defence of Portsmouth during the Second World War was an important one, its facilities having been developed in the 1930s for scheduled passenger services to and from London.

Sandown Airport (SZ 578841) has an interesting history. From 1929 to 1934 it was sited near Apse Manor Farm; one hangar is still used as a farm building (SZ 562818). In 1934 the airport was briefly sited between Ninham and Landguard Manor, but here nothing can be seen. In 1935 it moved to its present location, where it remained operational until the Second World War. After the war it was disused for a time; it is now in regular use for passenger traffic.

A most unusual site is at Totland (SZ 299848). It was here that the 'Black Arrow' and 'Black Knight' rockets were test-fired by the Saunders Roe Company during the 1950s. Although much of this complex has been lost, remains of some buildings survive;[26] one of the rockets has been preserved at the Scottish Museum of Flight at East Fortune, Lothian. The area around the test site is now owned by the National Trust.

Chapter Nine

Miscellaneous

The boundaries of what may be included as industrial heritage are very flexible. Some industrial historians would take a narrow view, but most would include agriculture, and probably public utilities. Dr. Riley, for instance, does not feel that the entertainment 'industry' or workers' housing should qualify,[1] and it is certainly problematic to know where to draw the line. The author, however, takes a broad view to include not just the conventional industries, but also examples which may be regarded as peripheral. This chapter will include many of these marginal cases which may, nevertheless, be considered to have contributed to our industrial heritage.

Communications

Admiralty Telegraphs The earliest system of telegraphic communications in Hampshire was that devised by Lord George Murray in the closing years of the 18th century. Of this nothing tangible remains, although the sites of some of the wooden buildings are marked by road names such as Telegraph Lane.[2] The only survivals are some of the telegraph stations which formed part of the London to Plymouth line, built between 1829 and 1831. This was a semaphore system, used to relay orders and reports from Whitehall to Admiralty outposts and to convey messages back. It was finally replaced at the end of 1847 by the electric telegraph. The buildings which survive are of varying height, depending on the needs of the line of sight. Each structure was similar, though, having a flat roof through which passed a mast bearing two semaphore arms, operated from a room beneath. One of the best can be seen at Four Marks (SU 680347), where the single-storeyed telegraph house has been converted to a dwelling. At Binsted (SU 785414), a taller building was required and a distinctive three-storeyed structure remains, much altered. Other stations have fared less well: that at Cheesefoot Head (SU 523281) has been demolished, but the site can be identified in a small copse; at Farley (SU 397275), the single-storey building is now in a very derelict condition.

Lighthouses Although lighthouses had been erected along the coastline for many centuries to aid navigation, it was not until the 18th century that a systematic approach to their design was considered. Most now rely on electricity for power instead of the oil used in the past. The principle, however, is similar: a magnified light, with a shutter revolving round it, produces a regular signal which identifies the lighthouse to vessels.

Several lighthouses may be seen on the coasts of Hampshire and the Isle of Wight. At Southsea (SZ 613981) a tower 34 feet high on the walls of the Castle gives an elevation for the lantern of 51 feet. Dating from 1823, it was erected by the Admiralty. At Hurst Point, the situation is more complex (SZ 318899-317898). Five lighthouses have stood on the site, of which three survive. The present high lighthouse, a white painted circular brick tower, is 85 feet high, and dates from 1868. The low light of the same date, a 54-foot high tower of unfaced brick, can still be seen, but is disused. The lighthouse which replaced this, built in 1911 and still in use, is a square tapering sheet steel structure painted red. The two earlier lights were removed during the 1860s when alterations were made to Hurst Castle.

On the Isle of Wight, the octagonal stone building on St. Catherine's Hill (SZ 493772), known as the Salt Pot, is of 14th-century date and, although long disused, is one of the

88. Saltpot (former lighthouse) on St Catherine's Hill, Isle of Wight.

oldest surviving lighthouses in Britain. St. Catherine's Lighthouse (SZ 498753) dates from 1840, and is now lit by electricity from its own generator, although until the 1880s oil lamps were used. It is now 77 feet high, reduced from 120 feet to ease problems caused by fog.

An important island lighthouse is that of the Needles (SZ 289848). It is on an artificially cut platform on the outermost rock near sea level, and dates from 1859, although there has been a lighthouse at the Needles since 1785. The present light is electrically powered, using its own generator.

Not a lighthouse, but equally an aid to shipping, is Ashey Down Seamark (SZ 575875). This 20-foot high triangular pillar was erected in 1735 to ease the navigation of vessels up to Brading Quay (see Chapter 8).

Post Boxes Many pillar boxes of historic interest survive in Hampshire and on the Isle of Wight. At Morn Hill, Winchester (SU 494295), at Green Lane, Shanklin (SZ 582823) and at Melville Street, Sandown (SZ 596841), examples can be seen of a relatively uncommon design of post box, dating from 1936 and bearing the cypher of King Edward VIII. Victorian boxes of various types can be found, including a very early one, dating from c.1860 at Worlds End, Hambledon (SU 633123). At Gosport, outside the former railway station (SU 614002), stands a beautifully restored Penfold hexagonal pillar box of ornate design. It was supplied by Cochrane, Grove and Co. of Dudley. Perhaps the most unusual survival, though, is at Fritham (SU 232143), where there is a 19th-century post box erected by Schultze's for their workmen at the Gunpowder Works. It was renovated by the Forestry Commission in the mid-1970s.

A most unusual telephone box can be seen at Bembridge, Isle of Wight (SZ 645883), constructed of concrete and wood, with a very ornate roof.

The Corset Industry

The manufacture of corsets, which flourished in Portsmouth in the 19th century and continues on a small scale today, is an unexpected industry for Hampshire. The remains are rather unimpressive when compared with, say, the Dockyard, yet the industry employed, by 1900, more than 2,000 people in the town.[3] It began as a 'putting-out' system, with sailors' wives and widows among others working at home, which reduced the overheads for the entrepreneurs.[4] Later the system was replaced by factories, and remains of a number of these may be seen, though the industry has contracted considerably since the Second World War.

In Goldsmith Avenue (SZ 657998) there is a factory built in 1921 which until recently, although re-used, was little altered,but has now undergone fairly major change. The Marina Factory, Southsea (SZ 662989), dating from 1897, is a two-storey building with typically large windows and a clerestory at the apex of the roof.[5] The Hampshire Corset Company,

90. Post box, Gosport.

89. Edward VIII post box, Sandown, Isle of Wight.

91. Telephone box at Bembridge on the Isle of Wight.

established in 1899 in Fratton Road (SU 650015), is still in operation, using mainly modern plant but also some hand machines.[6]

Storage

Warehouses Many fine warehouse buildings, particularly in Portsmouth and Southampton, were lost as a result of enemy action in the Second World War, or have been converted for other purposes, such as those at Newport Quay (See Chapter 8). One surviving example is the impressive Geddes Warehouse in Southampton (SU 419110). Six storeys high, it dates from 1866, although it incorporates a late 18th-century Customs baggage warehouse. It is now used as a restaurant and apartments, being part of the redevelopment which has taken place in the Town Quay area of the city.

92. Geddes Warehouse, Southampton.

Icehouses Before the invention first of ice-making machines and then of the modern refrigerator, ice was stored in specially constructed buildings to preserve food. The use of ice dates from as early as the 4th century B.C.,[7] although its introduction to England as a method of preserving food came much later.[8] By the late 18th century almost every country house had its ice-house in the grounds, and it is the remains of these that can still be seen. Ice was also imported for use in the wholesale and retail trades, although of the special warehouses built in Portsmouth and Southampton none survives. The ice-houses connected with country houses are often derelict and over-grown, and great care is needed when looking for them. In Hampshire there are remains of more than 40 icehouses[9] of which an excellent example is that at Mottisfont Abbey (SU 327270). The National Trust, who own the property, have recently cleared and restored it, and it is now open to the public (see Appendix 2). It is a fairly typical example, approached by a passage 8ft. 4ins. long, with a square drain at the bottom of the pit. At Westbury House, West Meon (SU 658238), there are two adjacent icehouses which, although they contain some rubbish, are in a fairly good state of preservation, with wing walls leading to the entrances. Another example in good repair is that at Fairfield House, Hambledon (SU 648154), which has been cleaned out to reveal the construction of the drain at the bottom of the pit.

On the Isle of Wight there is a very overgrown icehouse, with a domed roof, in the grounds of Appuldurcombe House (SZ 541800); it is not normally open to the public.

Entertainment

Theatres, cinemas and bandstands are some of the structures of interest to the industrial historian. Several historic Hampshire theatres are currently undergoing restoration or have recently been renovated. In Portsmouth, the Theatre Royal (SU 640000) was rebuilt in 1900 on the site of a previous theatre. Its architect was Frank Matcham, and at the time its stage was one of the largest in England. It is a very fine building and work has been taking place on both the interior and exterior to restore its former glories after years of disuse and a disastrous fire. Its iron facade, which projects over the pavement, has a round-arched colonnade supported by pairs of Ionic columns, with an enclosed balcony above; the decorative ironwork is particularly beautiful.[10] Another of Matcham's theatres is the King's Theatre at Southsea (SZ 648990), which dates from 1907. This has remained in use and retains its Edwardian character – a good example of the period.

93. King's Theatre, Southsea.

In Winchester, the Theatre Royal (SU 481297) was for many years a cinema. Recently extensive renovation has taken place, and it is once more used for live performances.

The number of cinemas has declined dramatically in recent years and as a result, they have attracted the notice of historians. Many of the buildings have been re-used; others have been demolished. In Southampton, several early cinemas survive. Of these the Atherley (SU 404134), built in 1912, is a good example. It was always a progressive cinema, being the first in the city to show 'talkies' in 1930, and to install stereophonic sound. Now a bingo hall, it remains relatively little changed apart from the screen area and the loss of its awning. Of similar date, and re-used in the same way, is the Woolston Picture House, Southampton (SU 436111). Its exterior is attractive: flat-fronted with a semi-circular gable in the centre, flanked by four mock windows, each with a sculpted bust in a roundel above.

An early Portsmouth cinema is the Shaftesbury, built in 1910 (SU 650014). This, like so many, is now a bingo hall, but keeps its distinctive appearance with a temple-like dome which was once surmounted by a statue of Mercury. Of later date, but very unusual, is the former Palace Continental (SU 643000). It opened in 1921 and was designed by a local architect, A.E. Cogswell. It is 'back to front', which is to say that the screen was situated

94.   Bandstand at Ventnor on the Isle of Wight.

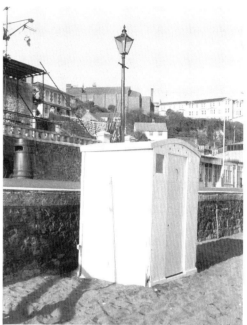

95.   Former Bathing Machine, Ventnor.

at the front of the building and the projection box at the rear. It is in a curious 'oriental' style, and now houses a nightclub.

A final example is the Plaza at Romsey (SU 358214), which stands on what was once the wharf of the Andover Canal (see Chapter 8). It has recently been restored for use as a theatre staging live performances.

On the Isle of Wight, the Shanklin theatre (SZ 583813) dates from 1933, and is impressively built in classical style with columns and pediment. Ventnor, like many resorts, had its Winter Gardens (SZ 565773) for the enjoyment of visitors, and the buildings on this site date from 1935. An earlier place of entertainment in the town is the Pavilion on the Esplanade (SZ 561774). This ornate building, now an amusement arcade, was erected in the late Victorian period for various functions such as concert parties. An interesting island cinema is the Rivoli at Sandown (SZ 598844), now used for bingo. Although relatively modern – dating from the 1930s – its art deco style makes it distinctive.

The bandstand is a Victorian relic which is increasingly coming back into use. That at Eastleigh (SU 455192), situated on the green near the Town Hall, came originally from Southampton. In Ventnor Park (SZ 555773) there is another; they almost invariably display ornate ironwork.

Seaside resorts have a heritage all their own, many retaining Victorian features. At Shanklin, several decorative shelters can be seen (for example at SZ 586814). At nearby Ventnor, former bathing machines survive, with their wheels removed and in some cases the bodies cut in two, now used as beach huts by longshoremen Blakes and Spencers (SZ 562774).

Retail Distribution and Administration

Public houses may be regarded as retail outlets, or for entertainment, and many have a

96. *The Pompey*, Fratton, Portsmouth.

97. Hurst shopfront, Ventnor, Isle of Wight.

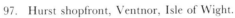

fascinating history and architecture. Portsmouth, as a naval port, had an unusually large number of them and a study can be rewarding in a number of ways![11] Even some small market towns contain a variety of interesting pubs: as early as the 1720s, Daniel Defoe described Petersfield as 'a town eminent for little, but its being full of good inns'.[12] At Romsey, too, the provision of public houses was prodigious: in 1911 there was one for every 141 inhabitants, almost twice the national average.[13]

A particularly attractive Portsmouth pub is *The Pompey* at Fratton (SZ 660999). Designed by Cogswell in c.1900, it is half-timbered, contrasting with the brown glazed brick on the ground floor. Also in Portsmouth, *The Mediterranean* in Stamshaw (SU 646023) has a beautiful mosaic depicting suitable scenes on a maritime theme. *The Old Drum* in Chapel Street, Petersfield (SU 745234) dates from at least the beginning of the 18th century, and has had several names, the present one being adopted in 1858.[14] At the beginning of this century it had an additional attraction in a bowling green.

The Isle of Wight also has a number of public houses of historic interest. *The Crab and Lobster* in Ventnor (SZ 563775) was the first licensed inn on the island and dates from the 18th century. Once thatched, it now has a slate roof and is situated next to the *King Charles I Hotel*. Nearby *The Hole in the Wall* (SZ 565775) is more than 200 years old and originally formed the coachmen's quarters of the *Central Hotel*, the actual stables being converted into what is now the Barn Bar.

Many historic shops have undergone drastic alteration, and good survivals are rare, apart from those in some villages. At Lymington there is a fine example in the High Street: formerly the premises of Messrs. Scats, it is now a shoe shop (SZ 326954). On the Isle of Wight a number of good Victorian shopfronts can be seen. Hursts ironmongers, in High Street, Ventnor (SZ 563775) has fine ironwork and has been little altered, while in Union Street, Ryde (SZ 592927) a number of shops date from the 1830s, although some have undergone some change. Buildings such as those in the Royal Victoria Arcade help retain the Victorian character of the area.

Once one includes in a study structures purpose-built for administration, a wide variety of buildings may be described. The

98. Prudential offices, Portsmouth.

Prudential building in Portsmouth (SU 640000) has already been mentioned in Chapter 4 in connection with the use of terracotta in its construction; it is also a fine example of a late Victorian office building. Designed by Waterhouse, it is four storeys high. The National Westminster Bank in High Street, Southampton (SU 420113) is an early example of a purpose-built bank, dating from 1867. It is possibly the best mid-Victorian building in the city, with Ionic columns and other intricate architectural detail. A point of historical interest concerning bank buildings is that until well into this century the manager was expected to live in accommodation provided above his bank. This was also true of many branch managers for retail chains, as will be mentioned in the section on workers' housing.

Many industrial historians would regard the heritage of the present century and certainly that of the post-war years as outside their area of study. It has to be remembered, however, that, with increasingly rapid change, relatively modern buildings are regarded as historic. A pioneer in the study of 20th-century industrial archaeology is Kenneth Hudson, who argues that 'the industrial history of our century is just as interesting and significant as that of the 150 years which preceded it':[15] a thought-provoking statement. Many of this century's industrial buildings have already been lost; it is therefore vital that those which remain are recorded and, where appropriate, preserved. One of the industries important in 20th-century history is that associated with computers, and already in Hampshire a major piece of computer archaeology exists. This is the former computer centre at the University of Southampton, which from 1958 until 1967 housed the University's first computer installations. The building (SU 424154) is now used as the University's Health Centre, and already many people in the University almost certainly have no idea of its former use.[16]

Workhouses

These buildings, the mention of which even now strikes fear into the hearts of many elderly people, are on the edge of industrial archaeology, but their inclusion can be justified on the basis that often inmates were put to work there. Many survive, frequently as geriatric hospitals: St. Christopher's Hospital, Wickham Road, Fareham (SU 579072) was built as the Union Workhouse in 1836. Of the same date, in Junction Road, Andover (SU 360457) is the impressive workhouse of red brick, two storeys high with nine bays.[17] In Portsmouth, the Portsea Union house was built in 1844 and designed by Livesay; once St. Mary's House, a geriatric unit, its future is at present uncertain (SU 661006). On the Isle of Wight at Newport, the local workhouse is now part of a hospital (SZ 496904).

Workers' Housing

This is probably the most difficult of all areas of industrial heritage to define. In a sense, if a strict limit were not adhered to, most housing would be so described – any dwelling where someone lived who was employed. For the purposes of industrial history the following definition is probably the most realistic: 'workers' housing is accommodation erected by or on behalf of an employer for employees of that company or undertaking'.

Using this definition, there are some very interesting examples in Hampshire and the Isle of Wight. Some linked with agriculture and defence supply have already been mentioned in Chapters 2 and 5. In some instances the houses doubled as home and workplace: crossing keepers' cottages, telegraph houses, and tollhouses among them. Another example is the lodge, to be found by the gates of many large estates. The lodge-keeper's task was to allow 'acceptable' visitors into the estate, as the security guard does today at the factory gate. A number of attractive lodges can be seen: at Uplands House, Fareham (SU 575075), the lodge's special feature is its set of ornamental chimneys. Another fine lodge is at Rotherfield Park (SU 701323) near Alton.

99.   Lodge of Uplands House, Fareham.

Other places where premises combined functions were railway stations, where often the
station master lived above the main station buildings – a good example is Woolston station
(SU 438113). Here, ground floor accommodation consisted of the booking office and waiting
rooms, with quarters for the station master above.[18] The provision of accommodation over
bank premises for branch managers has already been mentioned, and a similar policy
among many retail chains of literally 'living over the shop' continued until the 1950s.[19]

Most flour mills had a mill house, either in continuous range with, or adjacent to, the
mill. Two fine examples are those at Chesapeake Mill, Wickham (SU 574116), where a
most attractive mill house can be seen next to the mill, and the former Fareham Steam
Flour Mill (SU 579058). The latter was, incidentally, the first house in the town to be lit
by electricity, which was perhaps not surprising considering the proximity of the generating
station.

A number of employers provided accommodation. At Laverstoke a group of houses built
by the Portal family for their employees are of flint with red brick and in an attractive
Gothic design (SU 492485). Taskers, too, in the Anna Valley near Andover, erected 14
dwellings at Waterloo Terrace (SU 345439) for those employed at the ironworks. At Old
Burghclere (SU 470577) the urban type of houses for the limeworkers seems somewhat
incongruous in its rural setting. In other places, subsequent development has blended

rather better as at Riverview Terrace, Sarisbury (SU 499099), where houses were provided in the closing years of last century for employees at Bursledon brickworks.

At isolated locations, employers often built houses to attract labour to their works, as at Fritham where Schultze's Gunpowder Works was established. Eight cottages built in 1904 survive at what would be a safe distance from the works (SU 232140), together with a chapel also provided by the company.

Public utilities, too, often built company housing. To serve Twyford pumping station a number of houses can still be seen, together with the manager's house which is now in private ownership (SU 489247). At Mansbridge, where so little of the pumping station complex remains, a pair of houses associated with it still exist, (SU 447158). In Southampton, the Gas Light and Coke Company erected a block of flats for their workers in Britannia Road, Northam in 1900 (SU 431121). It was a condition of the lease that they should be occupied by 'persons of the labouring and artisan classes'.[20] The company regarded it as desirable that some employees should live within easy reach of the works to be called in if necessary.

Transport enterprises have a good record in general for the provision of workers' housing. In Eastleigh, the LSWR built a number of houses when the Carriage and Wagon Works and the Locomotive Works were moved down from London (see Chapter 5). Dutton Cottages (SU 493249) were built in 1892 for the company's firemen, and in 1899 houses were built in nearby Barton Road (SU 459191). The most impressive railway housing in Eastleigh is, however, the 175 terraced dwellings built on both sides of Campbell Road in 1909 (SU 457184). Another example is the two blocks of flats next to Fratton station, Portsmouth (SU 654001), which date from the late Victorian period, and are four storeys high, with four flats in each block. They have recently been renovated and are no longer owned by the railway.

The aircraft industry, too, often built houses for its employees. At Farnborough, eight terraces survive, dating from 1915, which were for workers at the Royal Aircraft Factory, now the Royal Aircraft Establishment. These dwellings, Pinehurst Cottages (SU 867549), are externally little changed. Also, at Hamble, a number of houses remain in Sydney and Vernon Avenues (for example at SU 461191) which were built for workers at the local aircraft factory.

Industrial Hamlet

Industrial settlements of major proportions such as Saltaire, near Bradford and New Lanark in Scotland are well-known. It is not generally realised, however, that in a quiet corner of Hampshire an industrial hamlet not only was built but still exists. This is at Hook, near Warsash (SU 510054).[21] It consisted of a smithy and house, a wheelwright's shop and house, and a terrace of four cottages for other workers. Outwardly it is little changed and retains its Victorian air, even though the wheelwright's shop has been converted into a restaurant and the smithy is now used for car repairs.

CONCLUSION

The aim of this book is to show just how much can be seen of the industrial heritage of Hampshire and the Isle of Wight. How deeply one chooses to study this, and the approach taken, is a matter of personal taste and circumstances. As Kenneth Hudson pointed out more than 20 years ago, industrial archaeology can, according to the individual concerned, 'be either a discipline or a pleasure, a means of adding to the world's store of knowledge, or a way of increasing one's personal awareness of the past'.[22] The stress placed on any particular aspect also varies: for some the history of technology is paramount, to others the architecture of the buildings which housed various pieces of machinery is of greater interest.

Some industrial historians believe it is vital that both buildings and machines should be viewed in their social context, and that the most fascinating area of study is the impact of industrialisation on people. Some may prefer a thematic approach, concentrating their interest for example, on transport, or mills. Others may specialise in particular geographical areas, or in such industrial archaeological concerns as the adaptive re-use of buildings, practical restoration work, or preservation schemes. In other words 'giving our past a future'.[23] As was suggested at the beginning of this book, industrial archaeology is sufficiently interdisciplinary to be 'a study to which everybody can bring some expertise . . . and expect to find a useful and rewarding field of investigation'.[24] It is hoped that the reader will have found this to be so.

Appendix One

Bibliography

GENERAL

Briggs, A., *Power of Steam* (1982)

Buchanan, R.A., *Industrial Archaeology in Britain* (1972)

Cossons, N., *The BP Book of Industrial Archaeology* (1987)

Defoe, D., *A Tour through the Whole Island of Great Britain* (1962 edn.)

Hudson, K., *Industrial Archaeology* (1963)

Hudson, K., *The Archaeology of the Consumer Society* (1983)

Mathias, P., *The First Industrial Nation* (1969)

Pannell, J., *Techniques of Industrial Archaeology* (1966)

Pannell, J., *An Illustrated History of Civil Engineering* (1964)

Raistrick, A., *Industrial Archaeology* (1972)

LOCAL

Cross, D., *The Story of Ringwood's Industries* (1963)

Insole, A. and Parker, A., *Industrial Archaeology in the Isle of Wight* (1979)

Monkhouse, F.J. (ed.), *A Survey of Southampton and its Region* (1964)

Moore, P., *A Guide to the Industrial Archaeology of Hampshire and the Isle of Wight*, S.U.I.A.G. (1984)

Moore, P., 'The Industrial Archaeology of Regions of the British Isles: No. 2 Hampshire' in *Industrial Archaeology Review*, vol. 8, no. 1 (1985)

Pevsner, N. and Lloyd, D., *The Buildings of England: Hampshire and the Isle of Wight* (1967)

Riley, R., 'The Industries of Portsmouth in the 19th Century', *Portsmouth Paper*, No. 25 (1976)

Riley, R., 'The Industrial Archaeology of the Portsmouth Region', *Portsmouth Paper*, No. 48 (1987)

Webb, J., Yates, N. and Peacock, S., (eds.), *Hampshire Studies* (1981)

The Making of Havant, Havant Local History Group (1977)

Old Romsey at Work, Lower Test Valley Archaeological Society (1976)

AGRICULTURE

Brigden, R., *Victorian Farms* (1986)

Chambers, J. and Mingay, G., *The Agricultural Revolution 1750-1880* (1969)

Course, E. and Moore, P., 'Victorian Farm Buildings in Hampshire'. *Proceedings of the Hampshire Field Club and Archaeological Society*, vol. 40 (1983)

Driver, A. and W., *A General View of the Agriculture of the County of Hants.* (1794)

Fowler, P., *Farms in England*, R.C.H.M. (1983)

Harvey, N., *The Industrial Archaeology of Farming in England and Wales* (1980)

Harvey, N., *A History of Farm Buildings in England and Wales* (1970)

Moore, P., 'Water Power on Brownwich Farm', *Industrial Archaeology Review*, vol. 7, no. 1 (1984)

INDUSTRIES BASED ON AGRICULTURAL PRODUCTS

Flour Milling

Ellis, M. (ed.), *Water and Windmills of Hampshire and the Isle of Wight*, S.U.I.A.G. (1978)

Major, J. Kenneth, *The Mills of the Isle of Wight* (1970)

Pelham, R., *Old Mills of Southampton*, Southampton Paper No. 3 (1963)

Reynolds, J., *Wind and Watermills* (1970)

Wailes, R., *The English Windmill* (1954)

Brewing
Lovett, M., *Brewing and Breweries* (1981)
Monckton, H., *The Story of British Beer* (1981)
Tighe, M., 'A Gazetteer of Hampshire Breweries', *Proceedings of the Hampshire Field Club and Archaeological Society*, vol. 27 (1970)

Textiles
Pelham, R., *Fulling Mills*, S.P.A.B. (undated)

Paper Manufacture
Coleman, D., *The British Paper Industry 1495-1860* (1958)
Shorter, A., *Water Paper Mills in England*, S.P.A.B. (1966)
Thomas, J.H., 'Warnford Paper Mill', *Industrial Archaeology*, vol. 5, no. 4 (1968)
Thomas, J.H., 'Hampshire and the Company of White Paper Makers', *Proceedings of the Hampshire Field Club and Archaeological Society*, vol. 26 (1969)

INDUSTRIES BASED ON MINERALS

Iron
Coppin, N., 'A Survey of Blacksmiths in Hampshire', *Proceedings of the Hampshire Field Club and Archaeological Society*, vol. 37 (1981)
Gale, W.K., *Iron and Steel* (1977)
Freeman, M., 'Funtley Iron Mill, Fareham', *Industrial Archaeology*, vol. 8 (1971)
Mott, R.A., (ed. P. Singer), *Henry Cort: The Great Finer* (1983)
Riley, R., 'Henry Cort at Funtley', *Industrial Archaeology*, vol. 8 (1971)

Brickmaking
Bricks and Brickmaking, Avoncroft Museum of Buildings (undated)
Hammond, M., *Bricks and Brickmaking* (1981)
White, W.C.F., 'A Gazetteer of Brick and Tile Works in Hampshire', *Proceedings of the Hampshire Field Club and Archaeological Society*, vol. 28 (1971)

Salt Manufacture
Lloyd, A., 'The Salterns of Lymington', *Proceedings of the Hampshire Field Club and Archaeological Society*, vol. 24 (1967)

Clay Pipes
Arnold, C., 'The nineteenth-century clay tobacco-pipe industry at Portchester', *Proceedings of the Hampshire Field Club and Archaeological Society*, vol. 31 (1974)

Glass Manufacture
Fox, R. and Lewis, E., 'William Overton and Glassmaking in Buriton', *Petersfield Monograph*, no. 1 (1982)

DEFENCE SUPPLY AND MANUFACTURING INDUSTRY

Coad, J., *Historic Architecture of H.M. Naval Base, Portsmouth 1700-1850* (1981)
Coad, J., *Historic Architecture of the Royal Navy* (1983)
Holland, A., *Ships of British Oak* (1971)
Morriss, R., *The Royal Dockyards during the Revolutionary and Napoleonic Wars* (1983)
Rance, A., *Shipbuilding in Victorian Southampton*, S.U.I.A.G. (1981)
Rance, A., (ed.), *Seaplanes and Flying Boats of the Solent*, S.U.I.A.G. (1981)
Riley, R., 'The Evolution of Docks and Industrial Buildings in Portsmouth Royal Dockyard 1698-1914', *Portsmouth Paper*, No. 44 (1985)
Riley, R., 'Portsmouth Dockyard: An Industrial Archaeological Overview', *Industrial Archaeology Review*, vol. 8, no. 2 (1986)

Rolt, L.T.C., *Waterloo Ironworks: A History of Taskers of Andover 1809-1968* (1969)
Whitehead, R., *Wallis and Steevens: A History* (1983)

PUBLIC UTILITIES

Gas
Barty-King, H., *New Flame* (1984)

Sewage
Course, E., *Eastney Pumping Station* (1975)

Water
Hallett, M., 'Portsmouth's Water Supply 1800-1860', *Portsmouth Paper*, No. 12 (1971)
Major, J. Kenneth, *Animal Powered Engines* (1978)

ROAD AND RAIL

Road
Addison, Sir William, *The Old Roads of England* (1980)
Albert, W., *The Turnpike Road System in England 1663-1840* (1972)
Bird, A., *Roads and Vehicles* (1969)
Copeland, J., *Roads and their Traffic 1750-1850* (1968)
Course, E., 'Portsmouth Corporation Tramways 1896-1936', *Portsmouth Paper*, No. 45 (1986)
Harrison, S.E., *Tramways of Portsmouth* (1955)
Horne, J.B., *100 Years of Southampton Transport* (1979)
Milton, A. and Bern, L., *Portsmouth City Transport 1840-1977* (1977)
Viner, D., 'The Industrial Archaeology of Hampshire Roads: A Survey', *Proceedings of the Hampshire Field Club and Archaeological Society*, vol. 26 (1969)

Rail
Course, E., *The Railways of Southern England, Volume One: The Main Lines* (1973)
Course, E., *The Railways of Southern England, Volume Two: Secondary and Branch Lines* (1975)
Course, E., *The Railways of Southern England, Volume Three: Independent and Light Railways* (1976)
Course, E., *Railways, Then and Now* (1979)
Course, E., 'Portsmouth Railways', *Portsmouth Paper*, No. 6 (1969)
Course, E., 'The Southampton and Netley Railway', *Southampton Paper*, No. 6 (1973)
Course, E. and Moore, P., *Hampshire Railways, Then and Now*, S.U.I.A.G. (forthcoming)
Robbins, M., *The Isle of Wight Railways* (1977)
Stone, R., *The Meon Valley Line* (1983)
Williams, R., *The London and South Western Railway, Volume I* (1968)
Williams, R., *The London and South Western Railway, Volume II* (1973)

WATER AND AIR

Water
Adamson, S., *Seaside Piers* (1977)
Course, E., *The Itchen Navigation*, S.U.I.A.G. (1983)
Course, E., 'Southampton Canal Tunnel', *Proceedings of the Hampshire Field Club and Archaeological Society*, vol. 33 (1976)
Hadfield, C., *The Canals of South and South-East England* (1969)
Horne, J.B., *Farewell to the Floating Bridges* (1977)
Paget-Tomlinson, E.W., *Canals and River Navigations* (1978)
Vine, P.A.L., *London's Lost Route to the Sea* (1965)
Vine, P.A.L., *London's Lost Route to Basingstoke* (1968)
Welch, E., 'The Bankrupt Canal', *Southampton Paper*, No. 5 (1966)
Williams, D., *Docks and Ports, I: Southampton* (1984)
A Souvenir of Southampton Docks (c.1930), reprinted S.U.I.A.G. (1982)

Air

Bagley, J.A., 'A Gazetteer of Hampshire Aerodromes', *Proceedings of the Hampshire Field Club and Archaeological Society*, vol. 29 (1972)

Coles, R., *A History of Beaulieu Airfield* (1982)

Molden, D., (ed.), *The Schneider Trophy Contest* (1981)

New, P.T., *The Solent Sky* (1976)

MISCELLANEOUS

Barker, J., Brown, R. and Greer, W., *The Cinemas of Portsmouth* (1981)

Course, E., 'Hook: An Industrial Hamlet', *Proceedings of the Hampshire Field Club and Archaeological Society*, vol. 39 (1983)

Ellis, M., *Ice and Icehouses through the Ages*, S.U.I.A.G. (1982)

Hague, D.D. and Christie, R., *Lighthouses* (1975)

Holmes, T., *The Semaphore* (1983)

Offord, J., *The Theatres of Portsmouth* (1983)

Riley, R. and Eley, P., 'Public Houses and Beerhouses in Nineteenth Century Portsmouth', *Portsmouth Paper*, No. 38 (1983)

Sargeant, H., 'A History of Portsmouth Theatres', *Portsmouth Paper*, No. 13 (1971)

'The Inns of Petersfield', *Petersfield Paper*, No. 3 (1977)

So Drunk He Must Have Been To Romsey, Lower Test Valley Archaeological Society (1974)

Museums in Hampshire and on the Isle of Wight containing items of Industrial Heritage Interest, and Sites Open to the Public

(Readers are advised to telephone before visiting, in case of changes in opening hours)

ALDERSHOT
  Royal Corps of Transport Museum (Mon.-Fri., 9-12, 2-4.30) Aldershot 24431, ext. 2417
ALTON
  Curtis Museum and Allen Gallery (Tues.-Sat., 10-5) Alton 82802
ANDOVER
  Andover Museum (Tues.-Sat., 10-5) Andover 66283
BASINGSTOKE
  Willis Museum (Tues.-Fri., 10-5; Sat., 10-4) Basingstoke 465902
BASINGSTOKE CANAL (Boat Trips)
  Telephone Fleet 5694
BEAUWORTH (Animal Wheel)
  The Milburys public house and restaurant. Bramdean 248
BOTLEY
  Hampshire Farm Museum (every day, 10-6) Botley 87055
BREAMORE
  Countryside Museum (April-Sept., afternoons except Mon. and Fri.) Downton 22270
BUCKLERS HARD
  Maritime Museum etc. (Easter-Sept., 10-6; Sept.-Easter, 10-5) Bucklers Hard 203
BURSLEDON WINDMILL
  Not open regularly yet: please contact Hampshire Buildings Preservation Trust in writing for permission to visit. See Appendix 3.
BUTSER
  Ancient Farm (Easter-end Oct., weekday afternoons, all day Sunday) Portsmouth 598838
EASTLEIGH
  Museum, High Street (Tues.-Fri., 10-5; Sat., 10-4) Southampton 643026
EASTNEY
  Pumping Station (April-Sept., 1.30-5.30, in steam at weekends; Oct.-Mar., first Sun. of month only, 1.30-5.30) Portsmouth 827261
ELING
  Tide Mill (Easter-end Sept., Wed.-Sun., 10-4. Closed Oct. Nov.-Easter, weekdays only, 10-4) Totton 869575
FARNBOROUGH
  Royal Aircraft Factory Museum. Open occasionally by appointment; please write to enquire.
GOSPORT
  Naval Ordnance Museum (Mon.-Fri., 10-4, but contact first) Portsmouth 822351, ext. 44225
  Museum (Tues.-Sat., 9.30-5.30) Gosport 588035
  Froude Museum, A.M.T.E., Haslar. By written appointment only.
HAVANT
  Museum (Tues.-Sat., 10-5) Havant 541155
HYTHE
  Pier Railway. Telephone for times. Hythe 843203

MIDDLE WALLOP
  Museum of Army Flying (daily, 10-4.30) Andover 62121, ext. 421
MID-HANTS. RAILWAY
  (Services Mar.-Oct. and Dec., weekends. Telephone for times) Alresford 734200
MOTTISFONT ABBEY
  Icehouse (Apr.-end Sept., Sun.-Thurs., 2.30-6) Romsey 40757
OWER
  Paulton's Park, restored sawmill (Apr.-Aug., 10-7; Sept. and Mar., 10-6; Oct.-Feb., 10-4.30)
  Southampton 814442
PORTSMOUTH
  Museum (daily, 10.30-5.30) Portsmouth 827261
SOUTHAMPTON
  Hall of Aviation (daily except Monday, 10-5) Southampton 635830
  Maritime Museum (Tues.-Sat., 11-1, 2-5, Sun., 2-5) Southampton 23941
SOUTHSEA
  Castle (daily, 10.30-5.30) Portsmouth 827261
SOUTHWICK
  Golden Lion Brewhouse (By appointment; ring curator) Cosham 380978
TWYFORD
  Pumping Station (By appointment only, plus open days as advertised. Contact Administrator: 10, High
  Firs Gardens, Romsey, SO51 8QA) Romsey 522842
WHITCHURCH
  Silk Mill (Mill shop, visitor centre and tea room open during working hours) Whitchurch 892065
WINCHESTER
  Museum (Apr.-Sept., daily; Oct.-Mar., daily except Mondays) Winchester 68166
  City Mill (Apr.-Oct., Tues.-Sat., afternoons; other times by special arrangement) Winchester 3723

ISLE OF WIGHT
ARRETON MANOR
  National Wireless Museum (Easter-Oct., Mon.-Fri., 10-6; Sun., 12-6; closed Sat.) Newport 528134
BEMBRIDGE
  Windmill (Apr.-Sept., daily except Sat.; open every day July and Aug.) Isle of Wight 873945
CARISBROOKE CASTLE
  Donkey Wheel (opening times vary; please telephone) Newport 3112
HAVENSTREET
  Railway (telephone for details of service) Wootton Bridge 882204
UPPER CALBOURNE
  Watermill (open daily in summer) Calbourne 227
VENTNOR
  Longshoremen's Museum, The Esplanade (open daily in summer; check by telephoning) Ventnor
  852176 or 853176
YAFFORD
  Watermill (Apr.-Oct., 10-6) Brighstone 740610

Although not in the area covered by this book, the following are of particular interest for exhibits about industrial heritage:

AMBERLEY (Sussex)
  Chalkpits Industrial History Centre (Apr.-Oct., Wed.-Sun., and Bank Holidays) Bury 370
SINGLETON (Sussex)
  Weald and Downland Open Air Museum (Telephone for details) Singleton 348

Useful Addresses

Association for Industrial Archaeology
The Wharfage,
Ironbridge,
Telford,
Shropshire TF8 7AW

Southampton University Industrial Archaeology Group
The Secretary,
c/o Department of Adult Education,
The University,
Southampton,
Hampshire SO9 5NH

Council for British Archaeology, Group 12
The Secretary,
c/o Salisbury Museum,
The Close,
Salisbury,
Wiltshire

Hampshire Field Club and Archaeological Society
The Secretary,
c/o Department of History,
King Alfred's College,
Winchester,
Hampshire

Hampshire Buildings Preservation Trust
c/o The Castle,
Winchester,
Hampshire

Historic Farm Buildings Group
c/o The Secretary H.F.B.G.
Museum of English Rural Life,
University of Reading,
Reading,
Berkshire

References

CHAPTER 1
1. Buchanan, R.A., *Industrial Archaeology in Britain* (1972), p. 19
2. Cossons, N., *The BP Book of Industrial Archaeology* (2nd edn. 1987), p. 10
3. Defoe, Daniel, *A Tour through the Whole Island of Great Britain* (1962 edn.), vol. 1, p. 142

CHAPTER 2
1. Chambers, J.D. and Mingay, G.E., *The Agricultural Revolution 1750-1880* (1969), p. 5
2. *ibid.*, p. 180
3. *ibid.*, p. 181
4. Driver, A. and W., *General View of the Agriculture of the County of Hants.* (1794), p. 19
5. Moore, P., 'Water Power on Brownwich Farm', *Industrial Archaeology Review*, vol. 7, no. 1 (1984), pp. 24-31
6. Harvey, N., *The Industrial Archaeology of Farming in England and Wales* (1980), p. 134
7. *ibid.*, pp. 136-7
8. Riley, R.C., 'The Industrial Archaeology of the Portsmouth Region', *Portsmouth Paper* No. 48 (1987), p. 13
9. I am indebted to Mr. C.J. Silman for this information
10. I am indebted to Mr. C.J. Silman for this information
11. I am indebted to Mr. A.C. Yoward for this information

CHAPTER 3
1. Reynolds, J., *Windmills and Watermills* (1970), p. 9
2. *ibid.*, p. 69
3. *ibid.*, p. 69
4. Wailes, R., *The English Windmill* (1954), p. 153
5. Ellis, M. (ed.), *Wind and Watermills in Hampshire and the Isle of Wight*, Southampton University Industrial Archaeology Group (1978)
6. *ibid.*, p. 4
7. Monckton, H.A., *The Story of British Beer* (1981)
8. Tighe, M.F., 'A Gazetteer of Hampshire Breweries', *Proceedings of the Hampshire Field Club and Archaeological Society*, vol. 27 (1970), p. 88
9. *ibid.*, p. 87
10. Defoe, *op. cit.*, p. 142
11. Major, J. Kenneth, *The Mills of the Isle of Wight* (1970), p. 58
12. Thomas, J.H., 'Hampshire and the Company of White Paper Makers', *Proceedings of the Hampshire Field Club and Archaeological Society*, vol. 26 (1969), p. 137
13. *The Making of Havant*, Havant Local History Group (1977), p. 10
14. Coleman, D.C., *The British Paper Industry, 1495-1860* (1958), p. 163
15. Thomas, *loc. cit.*, p. 137
16. Coleman, *op. cit.*, p. 68
17. Ellis, *op. cit.*, p. 52
18. Shorter, A.H., *Water Paper Mills in England*, SPAB (1966), p. 8
19. Thomas, J.H., 'Warnford Paper Mill, Hampshire', *Industrial Archaeology*, vol. 5, no. 4 (1968), p. 394
20. Ellis, *op. cit.*, p. 7
21. I am indebted to Professor Alan Crocker for this information
22. Coleman, *op. cit.*, p. 305
23. Major, *op. cit.*, pp. 61-2
24. Riley, *op. cit.*, pp. 18-19

CHAPTER 4

1. I am indebted to Peter Singer for this information
2. The author holds a photocopy of the map in question
3. Bartlett, A.B., 'The Ironworks at Sowley in the Manor of Beaulieu, c.1600-1820' (1973), unpublished paper
4. Mott, R.A. (ed. P.Singer), *Henry Cort: The Great Finer* (1983), p. 26
5. *ibid.*, p. 27
6. His story is told in Mott, R.A. (ed. P. Singer), *op. cit.*
7. Riley, *op. cit.*, p. 5
8. The site has twice been excavated, in the 1960s by S. Weeks and N. Davies, and a decade later by Peter Singer (report not yet published). See also Freeman, M.D., 'Funtley Iron Mill, Fareham', and Riley, R.C., 'Henry Cort at Funtley' in *Industrial Archaeology*, vol. 8, pp. 63-76
9. Lloyd, A.T., 'The Salterns of the Lymington Area', *Proceedings of the Hampshire Field Club and Archaeological Society*, vol. 24 (1967), p. 86
10. *ibid.*, p. 96
11. Defoe, *op. cit.*, p. 206
12. *Bricks and Brickmaking*, booklet published by Avoncroft Museum of Buildings, p. 10
13. White, W.C.F., 'A Gazetteer of Brick and Tile Works in Hampshire', *Proceedings of the Hampshire Field Club and Archaeological Society*, vol. 28 (1971), p. 83
14. *Bricks and Brickmaking*, *op. cit.*, p. 10
15. *ibid.*, p. 12
16. White, *loc. cit.*, p. 84
17. *ibid.*, p. 81
18. Arnold, C.J., 'The nineteenth-century clay tobacco-pipe industry at Portchester, Hants.', *Proceedings of the Hampshire Field Club and Archaeological Society*, vol. 31 (1974), pp. 43-52
19. Insole, A. and Parker, A., *Industrial Archaeology in the Isle of Wight* (1979), p. 15
20. Fox, R. and Lewis, E., *William Overton and Glassmaking in Buriton*, Petersfield Monograph no. 1, Petersfield Historical Society (1982)

CHAPTER 5

1. Rance, A.B., *Shipbuilding in Victorian Southampton*, S.U.I.A.G. (1981), p. 8
2. Rance, A.B. (ed.), *Seaplanes and Flying Boats of the Solent*, S.U.I.A.G. (1981), p. 3
3. Moore, P. (ed.), *A Guide to the Industrial Archaeology of Hampshire and the Isle of Wight*, S.U.I.A.G. (1984). p. 55
4. Course, E., *The Railways of Southern England, Volume One: The Main Lines* (1973), p. 262
5. Robbins, M., *The Isle of Wight Railways* 1977), p. 8
6. Cross, D.A.E., *The Story of Ringwood's Industries* (1963), p. 6
7. *ibid.*, p. 8
8. Whitehead, R.A., *Wallis and Steevens – A History* (1983), p. 9
9. *ibid.*, pp. 53-82
10. Riley, R.C., 'The Evolution of Docks and Industrial Buildings in Portsmouth Royal Dockyard 1698-1914', *Portsmouth Paper*, No. 44, p. 3
11. Coad, J., *Historic Architecture of HM Naval Base Portsmouth 1700-1850*, Portsmouth R.N. Museum in conjunction with the Society for Nautical Research (1981), p. 6
12. Riley, *Portsmouth Paper*, No. 48, *op. cit.*, p. 3
13. *ibid.*
14. Coad, *op. cit.*, p. 17
15. Defoe, *op. cit.*, p. 136
16. *ibid.*, p. 137
17. *ibid.*, p. 138
18. Coad, *op. cit.*, p. 17
19. Riley, *Portsmouth Paper*, No. 44, *op. cit.*, pp. 7, 10
20. *ibid.*, p. 11
21. Coad, *op. cit.*, p. 12

22. Riley, *Portsmouth Paper*, No. 44, *op. cit.*, pp. 12-13, and Riley, R.C., 'Portsmouth Dockyard: An Industrial Archaeological Overview', *Industrial Archaeological Review*, vol. 8, no. 2 (1985), pp. 177-93
23. Riley, *Portsmouth Paper*, No. 48, *op. cit.*, p. 11, and Riley, *Portsmouth Paper*, No. 44, *op. cit.*, pp. 13-14
24. Riley, *Portsmouth Paper*, No. 44, *op. cit.*, p. 16
25. *ibid.*
26. *ibid.*, p. 22
27. *ibid.*, p. 27
28. Riley, *Portsmouth Paper*, No. 48, *op. cit.*, p. 4
29. *ibid.*, p. 13
30. *ibid.*, p. 17

CHAPTER 6
1. Barty-King, H., *New Flame* (1984), pp. 13-15
2. Cossons, *op. cit.*, pp. 298-9
3. Riley, *Portsmouth Paper*, No.48, *op. cit.*, p. 20
4. Briggs, A., *The Power of Steam* (1982), p. 174
5. Moore, *op. cit.*, p. 44
6. Quoted in Course, E., *Eastney Pumping Station*, Portsmouth City Museums (1975), unpaginated.
7. Riley, *Portsmouth Paper*, No. 48, *op. cit.*, p. 20
8. *The Hampshire Telegraph and Sussex Chronicle*, 14 May 1887
9. Riley, *Portsmouth Paper*, No. 48, *op. cit.*, p. 20
10. *ibid.*, p. 21
11. Course, *Eastney Pumping Station*, *op. cit.*, unpaginated
12. Monkhouse, F.J. (ed.), *A Survey of Southampton and its Region* (1964), p. 98
13. Hallett, M., 'Portsmouth's Water Supply 1800-1860', *Portsmouth Paper*, No. 12 (1971), pp. 10-18
14. Riley, *Portsmouth Paper*, No. 48, *op. cit.*, p. 19
15. *ibid.*
16. *ibid.*, pp. 19-20, and Moore, *op. cit.*, pp. 35-6
17. Major, J. Kenneth, *Animal Powered Engines* (1978), p. 15
18. *ibid.*, p. 108
19. *ibid.*
20. *ibid.*, p. 111

CHAPTER 7
1. Addison, Sir William, *The Old Roads of England* (1980), p. 87
2. *ibid.*, pp. 97-8
3. Albert, W., *The Turnpike Road System in England 1663-1840* (1972), p. 26
4. *ibid.*, p. 43
5. *ibid.*, p. 45
6. Moore, *op. cit.*, p. 44
7. Viner, D., 'The Industrial Archaeology of Hampshire Roads: A Survey', *Proceedings of the Hampshire Field Club and Archaeological Society*, vol. 26 (1969), pp. 155-72
8. Moore, *op. cit.*, p. 45
9. Milton, A.F. and Bern, L.T.A., *Portsmouth City Transport 1840-1977* (1977), p. 1
10. Course, E., 'Portsmouth Corporation Tramways 1896-1936', *Portsmouth Paper*, No. 45, p. 3
11. *ibid.*, p. 9
12. *ibid.*, p. 17
13. Horne, J.B., *100 Years of Southampton Transport* (1979), p. 4
14. *ibid.*, p. 10
15. Insole and Parker, *op. cit.*, p. 35
16. Williams, R., *The London and South Western Railway*, vol. 1 (1968), p. 17
17. Course, E., *The Railways of Southern England, Volume Two: Secondary and Branch Lines* (1974), p. 210
18. *ibid.*, pp. 203 ff
19. Course, E., *The Railways of Southern England, Volume One: The Main Lines* (1973), p. 159

20. *ibid.*, p. 256
21. Williams, R., *The London and South Western Railway*, vol. 2 (1973), p. 90
22. Course, E., *The Railways of Southern England, Volume Three: Independent and Light Railways* (1976), p. 20
23. Course, *op. cit.*, vol. 2, pp. 228-36
24. *ibid.*, p. 232
25. *ibid.*
26. Course, E. and Moore, P., *Hampshire Railways Then and Now*, S.U.I.A.G., (forthcoming)
27. Robbins, *op. cit.*, p. 6
28. *ibid.*, p. 5

CHAPTER 8

1. Hadfield, C., *The Canals of South and South-East England* (1969), p. 171
2. Welch, E., *The Bankrupt Canal*, Southampton Papers No. 5 (1966), p. 19
3. *ibid.*, p. 21
4. Course, E., 'Southampton Canal Tunnel', *Proceedings of the Hampshire Field Club and Archaeological Society*, vol. 33 (1976), pp. 73-8
5. Hadfield, *op. cit.*, p. 141
6. *ibid.*, p. 142
7. Riley, *Portsmouth Paper*, No. 48, *op. cit.*, p. 14
8. Course, E., *The Itchen Navigation*, S.U.I.A.G. (1983), p. 5
9. Told in Course, *The Itchen Navigation*, *op. cit.*
10. Defoe, *op. cit.*, p. 186
11. Hadfield, *op. cit.*, pp. 152-3
12. Defoe, *op. cit.*, p. 141
13. *A Souvenir of Southampton Docks*, repr. by S.U.I.A.G. (1982), p. 5
14. Williams, R.L. *Docks and Ports, 1: Southampton* (1984), p. 36
15. *ibid.*, p. 38
16. *ibid.*, p. 40
17. Riley, *Portsmouth Paper*, No. 48, *op. cit.*, p. 10
18. Insole and Parker, *op. cit.*, p. 41
19. Adamson, S., *Seaside Piers* (1977), p. 110
20. Bagley, J.A., 'A Gazetteer of Hampshire Aerodromes', *Proceedings of the Hampshire Field Club and Archaeological Society*, vol. 29 (1972), p. 94
21. *ibid.*, p. 98
22. *ibid.*, p. 103
23. *ibid.*, p. 100
24. *ibid.*, p. 99
25. *ibid.*, p. 101
26. Insole and Parker, *op. cit.*, p. 21

CHAPTER 9

1. Riley, *Portsmouth Paper*, No. 48, *op. cit.*, p. 3
2. See Moore, *op. cit.*, p. 69
3. Riley, R., 'The Portsmouth Corset Industry in the Nineteenth Century', in Webb, J., Yates, N. and Peacock, S. (eds.), *Hampshire Studies* (1981), p. 245
4. *ibid.*, p. 260
5. Riley, *Portsmouth Paper*, No. 48, *op. cit.*, p. 18
6. *ibid.*
7. Ellis, M., *Ice and Icehouses through the Ages*, S.U.I.A.G. (1982), p. 1
8. *ibid.*
9. *ibid.*, pp. 53-77
10. Pevsner, N. and Lloyd, D., *The Buildings of England: Hampshire and the Isle of Wight* (1967), p. 460
11. See Riley, R. and Eley, P., 'Public Houses and Beerhouses in Nineteenth Century Portsmouth', *Portsmouth Paper*, No. 38 (1983)

12. Defoe, *op. cit.*, p. 141
13. *So Drunk He Must Have Been to Romsey*, Lower Test Valley Archaeological Society (1974), p. 8
14. 'The Inns of Petersfield', *Petersfield Paper*, No. 3 (1977), p. 23
15. Hudson, K., *The Archaeology of the Consumer Society* (1983), p. 1
16. *ibid.*, pp. 110-11
17. Pevsner and Lloyd, *op. cit.*, p. 82
18. See Course, E., 'The Southampton and Netley Railway', *Southampton Paper*, No. 9 (1973), p. 21
19. The author was born in such accommodation, in the flat above Currys Ltd., Chapel Street, Petersfield (SU 746234).
20. See Moore, *op. cit.*, p. 41
21. See Course, E., 'Hook – an Industrial Hamlet', *Proceedings of the Hampshire and Archaeological Society*, vol. 39 (1983), pp. 223-30
22. Hudson, K., *Industrial Archaeology* (1963), p. 34
23. A most appropriate phrase, for which I am indebted to Michael Messenger
24. Buchanan, *op. cit.*, p. 19

Index